WILL I CRY TOMORROW?

Healing Post-Abortion Trauma

Susan M. Stanford, Ph.D.

WILL I CRY TOMORROW?

Healing Post-Abortion Trauma

with David Hazard

Fleming H. Revell Company
Old Tappan, New Jersey

Library of Congress Cataloging-in-Publication Data

Stanford, Susan.
  Will I cry tomorrow?

  "A Chosen book"—T.p. verso.
  Bibliography: p.
  1. Stanford, Susan.   2. Abortion—United States—
Biography.   3. Abortion—Religious aspects—
Christianity.   I. Hazard, David.   II. Title.
HQ767.5.U5S735   1986   363.4'6'0924   86-29822
ISBN 0-8007-1512-8

To Jeremy

CONTENTS

Contents

WILL I CRY TOMORROW?

Healing Post-Abortion Trauma

1
THE DECISION

I awoke to the fresh smell of a summer morning rain. A fine, steady shower tapped at my bedroom window, which was open just a crack. In the rest of the apartment all was quiet and I assumed that my roommate, Laura, was still asleep. Still half-asleep myself, I found that the sheet was clenched in my tight fists. From head to foot every muscle was tense and I felt exhausted, as though I hadn't had a full eight hours of sleep. My chest rose with a deep breath and I let it out slowly trying to relax.

And in that moment, as I awoke fully, I knew what day this was: Tuesday, the first of July. At nine o'clock, I was to be at the clinic for my appointment. Raising myself on one elbow, I thought, *I can still cancel.* Then, *No. I've got to go through with it.*

Pushing back the sheet, I let my feet land on the floor with a dull-sounding thud. Numb. Wooden. I had kept a tight lid over my feelings since I had made the appointment.

Hang onto the numbness, Susan, I counseled myself, reaching for my pink dressing gown. *It's the only thing that will get you through this.*

Rising, I made my way into the bathroom to take a shower. Breakfast was out of the question. Outside the apartment, I heard a car motor start as one of my neighbors set off early, probably trying to beat the heavy commuter traffic from Evanston into Chicago. I glanced out through the drizzle that streaked the bathroom window. Why did it have to be overcast and cool on top of everything else? The sky looked hard, like wet, gray cement, and I could tell that we were in for the all-day sort of rain that Lake Michigan dumps on northern Illinois so frequently.

Normally, I would be rushing to gather my papers, dab on a little makeup, and be off to the early-morning psychology class I was teaching at nearby Northwestern University. I had just graduated from the N.U. doctoral program that same spring of 1975 and was fortunate enough to land a job with the university immediately.

"Fortunate" isn't the word Frank would use, I reminded myself as I stepped from the shower. He had blamed most of the problems of our marriage on my being in that doctoral program, on my trying to pursue a meaningful career, on "all that women's lib stuff"—on anything but the real cracks that had come to riddle the foundation of our marriage. I had felt sure, several months before, that the only way to get him to listen to me, to hear my pleas, was to shock him by moving out temporarily.

If only it had worked. If only that were the full truth. I had to face myself with the fact, as I dressed and brushed my shoulder length dark hair into some semblance of order, that I had made unwise choices. In the mirror, I stared at the pale skin—so like my mother's English peaches-and-cream complexion—that made my dark, tired eyes look sunken. I had allowed myself to become too emotionally vulnerable, had spent far too much time painting Frank as the hard-hearted black knight. Yet how much I still loved Frank, and how I wanted our marriage to be mended.

If that's true, then why did you—? I shut my eyes and gripped the edge of the sink. I could hardly face my own reflection, let alone these thoughts. I had come from a good family, considered myself intelligent, well-bred. I fought down the scalding self-hatred.

I left the bathroom, took my umbrella out of the foyer closet, then stepped out into the slow, rhythmic rain. Getting into the car I kept up the mental dialogue, sounding so much like the cool, professional counselor, the psychology prof I had become. Yet the car key trembled in my hand and I could barely get it into the ignition. I managed somehow to get the car started, took a few more deep breaths, then pulled out of the parking lot.

As I drove, I continued the inner pep talk. I reminded myself that my emotions had gotten me into this mess and now I had to listen to the voice of reason if I wanted to get out of it. Regardless of my religious upbringing, regardless of my own feminine instincts, there seemed to be only *one* way out. And that was to go through with "the procedure" I was about to undergo.

Gripping the steering wheel, I maneuvered the wet streets of Evanston somehow as surges of inner chaos threatened to break through. Mentally, I seized my emotions. *Don't give in.* My own mind had become an enemy, accusing me and telling me what a fool I had been. Nights, I would lie awake imagining the shocked faces of my parents, my brothers, and family friends—and, of course, Frank. I couldn't think of the explosion if he found out, so I didn't think at all.

In fact, I had tried to deny my "problem" from the first moment. Stopping for a red light, I recalled the morning that I first discovered that my breasts were painful and slightly enlarged. I had always been athletic and I knew my body well, but I could not accept those first signs—that is, not until I missed a period. That had never happened. All at once I had been catapulted into a tangle of confusion: Frank and I were estranged, had not lived together in months; but I wanted reconciliation. How was I to manage that now? How could I drop in to see him and casually mention that I was one month pregnant?

My thoughts glanced lightly over that last word. The "thing" inside me had only been growing for a few weeks at the most. I had been raised Roman Catholic—it embarrassed me to recall—and I could not begin to think of that "thing" as a living being. In my best clinical voice, I had told myself not to get emotional, to phone a clinic immediately, and have the "lump of cells" removed.

I turned left at the next light and drove up a pleasant tree-lined drive into the clinic parking lot. *If this is just like any other surgical procedure—like having a cyst removed—then why did I give the appointment secretary a false name on the telephone?* As a professional I always encouraged my clients to accept responsibility for their own actions, but I had been unable to make an appointment in my own name, Dr. Susan Stanford. *And why did I panic when she said I'd have to wait because they were booked up for ten days?*

These inner jabs hurt. I had to keep myself from thinking, just for a little while longer—until it was all over. Switching off the ignition, I stared at the brick building before me. It was modern, clean, welcoming, and large. I would be inconspicuous here. Just another face. My palms were sweating and I fought against the watery, weak feeling that had rushed into my legs and arms. The rain had slowed and I stepped out of the car leaving my umbrella behind.

At the receptionist's desk I stood uncomfortably, waiting for the woman to finish a phone conversation. She glanced at me and I whispered, "I'm Sally Brown. I have a nine o'clock appointment." Without missing a beat she handed me a pen and a clipboard with a long form attached and motioned for me to fill it out.

Mechanically, I scratched the answers into the right spaces. When I returned the form she was off the phone. She smiled at me and said, "Now let me explain the process to you." First I would speak to a counselor. Then I would be taken to a room where they would perform the procedure. *The procedure.* It did not escape my attention that she avoided using the other word for it, just as I had. Afterward, I would rest in a recovery room until they were sure I was all right. The whole thing would take about three or four hours.

The receptionist then led me into a small private office to meet my counselor, a pretty blond woman of about thirty.

"I'm Julie," she said warmly, extending her hand to me. "Please have a seat, Sally. I'm going to spend a little time with you and discuss the procedure."

The procedure. I felt a little light-headed as she continued speaking. Her manner was gentle. I was thinking that this was no novice, nor a callous, jaded clinician. She seemed genuinely to care about me—Sally, or whoever I was. I focused on her delicately colored lips, trying not to let the ripples of emotion swell.

She was saying, "I'd like to help you process your feelings if I can."

"Okay." That was all I could manage. I felt my chin begin to tremble.

"How do you feel," she continued—and my eyes shifted from her face to the floor—"about your decision to have an abortion?"

I swallowed. My hands, resting in my lap, had become a blur. "I've thought a lot . . . I feel . . . it's an eighty/twenty sort of decision."

"What do you mean?" Julie pursued.

I opened my mouth to answer but only a sob escaped. I couldn't hold it together any longer. Tears splashed onto my clenched hands. I sobbed and sobbed and sobbed. In another moment, if I just let go, I would be entirely out of control.

Julie's voice reached me through the tilting emotions. "Sally, you seem very upset. Maybe we should postpone your procedure today. Why don't you go home and give this another week's thought? It seems to me that there is too much pain attached to what you're about to do."

My hands clenched tighter. I had built my case so strongly that this was the only way out for me. I could not wait another week, not even an hour. With a supreme effort, I closed the lid on my emotions and my feminine instincts. Cool reason had to take control.

I found my voice and replied, "No. I'm not going to postpone. Things have gotten too complicated for me. This will simplify matters so I can handle my life again. Allowing this pregnancy to continue is not an option." There. I had made it. My decision was firm. The lid was tightly in place again.

Julie nodded. Something in her smile said, "I think you're valiant. Let's get on with it."

I let out a deep breath and rose to follow her to the procedure room. She patted my arm and left me there. In a moment a nurse entered and handed me a hospital gown. "The physician will be with you in a few moments."

I slipped into the gown, sat down, and stared at the wall. The nurse had said "in a few moments." Why had her tone sounded so cool, so businesslike? In a few moments it would all be over. I could forget this day. I could get on with my life, with efforts to reconcile with Frank. Things would be normal again.

But things would not be normal for a long, long time. More than my baby would die in that room. And my own mental strength would not be able to give life where death had come.

It would take a power far greater than I had ever known.

I waited in silence, trying to think of nothing. It was futile. Flickers of memory pressed in on me as if my unconscious mind, against my will, was trying to make sense of it all: how I—who hated abortion, who detested secret affairs and people who lead double lives—how I had found myself in this place.

2
COMPASSION

It is one of those photo-album memories of childhood imprinted in my head: the way the cool northern light spilled through the windows of our large family home in the country town of St. Bruno, fifteen miles outside of Montreal. As a little girl, I would play in that light as it splashed across the carpet and gleaming hardwood floors.

Invariably, just at supper time, my father would walk in, the sun catching his well-polished leather-soled oxfords, and he would stoop and lift me in his arms. With three brothers, I was Daddy's girl, and as I looked into his gentle eyes I had no question that I was loved. Then he would squeeze me once and set me down on the carpet again, retreating to the kitchen where my mother was busily preparing dinner.

I was proud of my father. He was a physician and I knew even as a small child that he cared for people. Occasionally Mother took us to meet him at his office, and it made me feel important to see my father's name on the signplate: Ronald L. Stanford, M.D., Cardiologist. In the waiting room, I thumbed through the limp copies of magazines and watched the men and women seated around me, their faces grim with concern. One by one they would be ushered into Daddy's inner office. And when they emerged, pausing in the doorway for a final word with him, the grimness would be gone, replaced with looks of relief. My father did that for people. Then he would pat their shoulders and leave them with some final word of assurance. I felt that he must be a very special man because so many people trusted him.

Likewise, my mother, Veronica, seldom missed a chance to hug or encourage my brothers and me. She always carried with her a sense of warmth and a flair for activities that were both fun and instructional. When my love for horses became apparent in almost every one of my crayon drawings, she let me take horseback-riding lessons at a nearby stable. Mother also agreed readily with my father that a good education was important for us, and so I was enrolled at Sacred Heart Convent, a private Catholic school for girls in Montreal.

The sisters of Sacred Heart emphasized traditional "book learning," and gave special attention to teaching the social graces, which were important for every cultivated young lady in the 1950s. The school prided itself on turning out well-educated young women who were highly motivated to contribute to society. Class projects and lectures conveyed to us the sense that we were responsible to serve in the community. My parents encouraged me in academics and in athletics as well. As I reached high school, I continued with my riding lessons until I was accomplished enough to compete frequently in show jumping.

In fact it was at the riding stable, one day in 1963, that one of the most jarring events of my young life took place.

On a Saturday morning, Mother left me off at the stable. A number of students were already there, lugging saddles and bridles or grooming their horses. Mother's car had barely disappeared out of the parking lot when one of my riding companions, Danielle, walked up and seized my arm. Though we often rode together, we did not know each other well. Since I was fifteen and she was several years older, we rarely saw each other away from the stables and horse shows. That morning her face was pale and she said, "Susan, I've got to talk to you. Now. Alone."

When we reached the far side of one of the barns, she turned and there were tears in her eyes. Her voice quavered as she asked, "Your father's a doctor, right?"

"Yes."

"Well, I need to see him right away."

"Okay," I said. "But what's wrong?"

"I'm bleeding badly. I'm afraid I'm hemorrhaging."

I was stunned. Other than obviously being upset, Danielle looked fine to me. "What happened?"

Her eyes wandered away from mine. "Two months ago I had an abortion. I was four months pregnant at the time. Some quack did it in his office after hours one night, and I've been bleeding ever since. I'm afraid I'm dying."

Now I was shaking, too. I was scared and couldn't believe

what I was hearing. Abortions were illegal. And as the Catholic Church had taught me, it was wrong: It was murder.

As if she felt compelled to explain, she said, "I got pregnant one night when I was seeing a guy from Montreal. I didn't know what to do. He didn't want anything to do with me. So after four months I told my parents. My father went crazy. He threatened to shoot me if I didn't 'get rid of it.' "

I stood there gaping. I knew Danielle's father. He had seemed brusque to me, even rude. But I couldn't imagine a father treating his pregnant daughter so cruelly.

"So I want to see your father. This morning," she insisted, jogging me out of my tongue-tied amazement.

On the phone I told my father only that Danielle was "ill." He said to have her come to our home right away. We drove there in her car, and I'm sure Mother was surprised to see me home so soon. One look at Danielle though and she just smiled and said, "Hello, girls."

Dad greeted her cordially, that familiar look of concern in his eyes. He ushered her into his den, closed the door, and I could imagine him pointing her to the overstuffed armchair by the bookshelf.

As they conferred, I retreated to the kitchen with Mother where, in a lowered voice, I spilled out the incredible story. Mother only shook her head. "Poor thing," she said.

My father spoke with Danielle only a few minutes before the den door opened. There were a few quiet words between them, then she left. Mother looked at him questioningly but all he said was, "I'm having her admitted to the hospital immediately."

I spent the rest of the day around the house. That evening, my father asked to speak with me alone in his study. I tried to imagine, as I sat in the comfortable chair opposite him, how terrified and upset Danielle must have felt.

"You were a great help to your friend today, Susan," Dad began. "She is very sick. The fact that you called me immediately was important."

I was touched that there did not seem to be an ounce of judgment in his attitude toward Danielle. Then his next statement surprised me.

"While I hope that nothing like this ever happens to you, I trust that you know you could always come to your mother and me. We would understand."

It felt so awkward to be talking to my father about these things. Even then, in the so-called permissive '60s, sex was not talked about so openly. In fact, even my mother and I had not talked about things like illegitimate pregnancy or abortion. But I was taken by my father's knowledge and the calm with which he had handled Danielle. It was comforting to hear him say that he and my mother would stand by me through whatever crises I might face in life.

As I left the den, he slipped his arm around me and I hugged him tightly. "Thanks, Daddy."

Even though I'd been comforted by his words, I was still troubled by the day's events as I put on my nightgown and switched off the bedside lamp. In my brief prayers I especially remembered Danielle. Lying there in the dark, I tried to imagine how she must feel in a strange hospital bed. I wondered if her parents would even visit her, acknowledge her illness, or if she would have to go it alone.

It was all so troubling to me. Before that day, abortion had been a remote concept, something that "bad" people did. I could not imagine for a minute what Danielle must feel like. A "late bloomer" myself where boys were concerned, I hardly ever dated, let alone thought about sexual involvement. I was just glad, as I rolled over and pulled the blankets about me, that we had been able to help Danielle.

After about two months Danielle turned up again at the riding stables. Though we often rode together, we never talked about that experience. I was just as glad to pretend it had never happened.

Before long I was accepted at Loyola College in Montreal, and in the next three years my interest in the horse show circuit gave way to involvement in sororities, the campus newspaper, women's hockey, cheerleading, and a host of other activities. I soon lost track of Danielle altogether.

She did come to mind several times during my senior year at Loyola when I served as a Resident Assistant in my college dorm. In that capacity, girls would sometimes come to me with problems involving their roommates or their studies. On several occasions, they came with problems involving their relationships with men. By this time, males and I had finally discovered each other, though I never considered "sleeping around," as some college-aged people were inclined to do.

Inspired by the flower children's "summer of love" out in San Francisco, young people across the country were throwing off traditional morals and talking about "free sex" in that year of 1967. Not me. I continued to attend Mass every Sunday and hold onto my traditional Catholic values,

24

despite the fact that a lot of my classmates were mouthing the popular "God is dead" philosophy that permeated too many universities. Though my faith was actually quite routine, even somewhat mechanical, I must have conveyed a sense of stability, for occasionally a girl in my dorm would single me out and ask advice about her tangled sexual involvements. I never knew if I was much help, but I listened and I did care.

It was during that year that I felt a dawning interest in the counseling profession. It seemed so natural, after growing up in a household so full of concern for the well-being of others, that I should go into one of the caring professions.

One fall afternoon I stopped by the office of one of the best-liked counselors on campus, Father O'Neil. I asked if he had some free time and he encouraged me to sit down. Since he showed up at most of the sports events, plays, and concerts on campus, I had chatted with him often and felt as if he were an old friend.

"How can I help you, Susan?"

"I'm interested in the kind of work you do," I started. "I think I'd like a job where I can be helping people, and I like the environment of a college campus."

We talked at length about the pluses and minuses of his job. With his usual good humor, he told me about the headaches as well as the joys. As he talked, I found myself drawn into his world. It was obvious that he really cared about students. I probed his knowledge of the better graduate programs in Counseling Psychology and he agreed to call several friends he knew in the field and get their recommendations. At the end of our two-hour conversation, I left elated, with the feeling that I was about to make one of the most important choices of my life.

Shortly thereafter, Father O'Neil asked me to come to his office again. During his phone calls, one name had turned up again and again. Boston College was reputed to have one of the best programs in Counseling Psychology in the eastern United States. It didn't take long for the idea to sink in. I loved the thought of studying in Boston with its college-town atmosphere. Besides that I also loved the ocean, the mountains, and the good skiing that New England offered.

I sent an application to Boston College immediately and, in the spring semester of 1968, I was overjoyed to receive notice of my acceptance. I also applied for a job as "Head Resident" in one of the women's dorms, since it meant not only good work experience, but full tuition, room and board, and a small cash stipend. The college notified me promptly that the position was mine. I was to report one week before classes began in the fall.

So September 1968 saw me moving to Boston to pursue my Master's degree, aiming at a career in professional counseling. As I unloaded my suitcases and personal belongings into my dorm room, I was happy to think that I had easily made one of the most important career choices of my life. I had no way of guessing that Boston would also be the beginning of a paradoxically joy-filled yet pain-ridden relationship.

The group of "Head Residents" trained together for one week before classes started. We were taught to handle a broad array of situations, such as what to do if a fire broke out in our dorm, how to handle a student who might be suicidal, and how to carry out college policy when a resident was found to have a girlfriend or boyfriend staying over in his or her room. Besides that, campuses across the U.S. were being jostled by students and agitators protesting the Vietnam War. We had to know how to act with cool heads in the event of unrest or violence.

It was during that week of pre-school training that I met Frank Kelly, who was just beginning his last year at the law school. A good-looking man of average height, he had an amiable smile and a determined manner about him. We chatted on several occasions during the week and had our first date the following weekend.

We quickly discovered that we shared many similar interests. We were both avid sports enthusiasts. Dancing was a favorite common pastime. We'd both been raised Catholic, though he admitted that attending Mass was low on his list of priorities. He said he had once been engaged but, in his words, the relationship "just didn't work out."

Two weeks after arriving in Boston I was able to have my horse, Gray Dawn, shipped down from Montreal to a stable not far from the Boston College campus. I introduced Frank to her soon after she arrived. At first, he was a little timid around her since he'd never had any riding experience. But after a few lessons he felt comfortable enough in the saddle that we began to enjoy long weekend rides together through the New England countryside. I was thrilled to share this happy part of my life with Frank and see him take to it so readily, to feel that we were getting close.

We began to date frequently over the next seven or eight weeks. I met several of Frank's friends including Jim Smith, an attorney who soon became one of my own closest friends in Boston. As the fall winds off the harbor drove their chill into Boston the feelings between Frank and me seemed only to deepen. We'd often retreat to a small quiet restaurant near the Boston Common. While we talked, our eyes meeting over the steam from cups of clam chowder, Frank would slip his hand into mine and I would feel an exciting warmth rippling within.

I was amazed at how quickly and how deeply I fell in love with Frank Kelly. I had never felt so strongly about anyone in my life. From his words, from his kisses, I believed he felt the same way about me. Whenever we were not in class or attending to our dorm duties we were together either studying in the library or just taking long walks together on campus. It was the head-over-heels kind of love that made you do silly things.

For example, the three major snowstorms that hit Boston within four weeks that winter of 1969 didn't slow our involvement for a minute. The first storm dumped more than a foot of snow, paralyzing the city for days beneath unplowed streets. Classes were canceled. Frank was caught in his dorm on "the hill," where all the men's residences for the college were located, and I was trapped in my dorm blocks and blocks away in a grouping of buildings the school had bought after it went coed. The second storm was just as bad. Every day we talked for hours on the phone. Even so, I hated the fact that Frank and I were forced to be apart.

By the time the third storm hit I was determined. News bulletins on television and radio were warning Boston residents to stay in out of the blizzard. I looked out at the high-peaked snowdrifts that the 30- to 40-mile-an-hour winds were amassing beneath my dorm window. The longing to see Frank's smile, the desire to be held in his arms burned within. It was a foolish plan, I knew, but I picked up the phone and called him.

When he answered I led off with, "How would you like to meet me?"

"Susan? What are you talking about?" he replied, chuckling.

"I'm coming up to see you."

"You aren't. You *can't*. This blizzard is deadly."

"I'm coming."

"There are drifts in the roads."

"I'm putting my boots on right now."

"Susan, this is craziness—"

"I'll meet you in the library. Be there. I love you."

When we hung up, I put on long underwear under my corduroys, threw on my down-filled jacket, wrapped a scarf around my neck and over my knitted cap. Then I waddled downstairs and toward the door. When the R.A. on duty at the desk saw me, her mouth dropped open.

"Susan! You're not crazy enough to go out in this, are you?"

"I am," I laughed. "Don't wait up for me." I pushed open the door, and was nearly bowled over by a gust of wind-driven snow.

Pushing through the knee-deep snow, I trudged on, puffing as my legs grew weary. Tiny beads of ice whipped my face, but I made my way over South Street and up Commonwealth Avenue. After a full half-hour the lights of the library were in sight. The law school library had remained open for students with an overly developed scholastic urge.

Frank had had to trudge an almost equal distance to get there, and when we met just inside the doors, we burst out laughing. Frank's eyebrows were frosted over and we were both covered with snow from head to foot. It was like a scene from the movie *Dr. Zhivago* where the two lovers, driven by their desire, meet in a frozen hideaway.

Warming my cold hands between his, Frank whispered, "Susan, I love you more than you'll ever know." Then we made our way to a quiet, deserted study room downstairs. There, in each other's arms, we talked and laughed. We were oblivious to time passing, as only two lovers can be.

Two or three hours later, as we parted, I wrapped my scarf tightly around my face and, standing out in front of the library in the blinding blizzard, I did a crazy little dance for Frank. It became our silly signal to each other that we were too happy for words. Frank and I laughed so hard I thought we would fall into a snowbank.

As I trudged homeward, I felt as though I were walking on top of the snow instead of plowing through it. I could not believe that I had been blessed with so marvelous a love. I could imagine our lives intertwined forever in this enormous feeling that surged through me. That night as I lay in bed I prayed, telling God how grateful I was for the love I felt for Frank. At twenty-one I had found the most wonderful thing life could give: unbounded love.

Or so I thought.

3
NOT LIES,
JUST HALF-TRUTHS

One evening in late March a random phone call unexpectedly turned my world upside-down. I had telephoned our good friend Jim Smith to check on some weekend plans we had made to double date. During the course of the conversation, Jim started telling me about some of the zany things he and Frank had done together in the past.

While laughing at Jim's stories, I decided to ask him about a topic that had me naturally curious. "Say, Jim, tell me a little about Frank's former fiancée."

"As a matter of fact I didn't get to know her very well," Jim replied. "We really didn't spend a whole lot of time together while they were married."

In my head I corrected him. Of course he meant engaged. "Oh, come on," I pursued. "Tell me anything. Was she athletic? How did they meet?"

Jim rummaged about his memory enough to satisfy most of my questions. He told me that she and I were very different from each other, which made me feel good. I didn't want to be the look-alike or act-alike of some past, failed love affair. "But I can't tell you much more than that," Jim finished. "As I said, they kept to themselves while they were married."

"Jim," I said abruptly, "they weren't married. They were just engaged."

At the other end of the line I heard Jim gasp. In the silence that followed, I felt as if the floor were collapsing beneath my feet. Haltingly, Jim made a feeble attempt to recover. "Gosh, Susan, I'm sorry. I thought you knew everything."

I couldn't answer. The tears were streaming down my face. There was such a strong pain in my chest I could hardly breathe. I held the phone receiver away and wept, hearing Jim's voice, tiny and faraway, calling my name over and over. The man I loved with all my heart had lied to me. He had been married and was divorced. According to the teachings of my Church I would commit a mortal sin if I were to marry him. Frank was Catholic too. He knew the implications of his divorce. My head was bursting with questions. Why hadn't he told me?

Finally, I lifted the receiver again. Through tears I managed: "Jim, I need to talk with you. Can I come over?"

"Sure, Susan." He sounded just as devastated as I felt. "Come on over."

How I drove myself to Jim's apartment in Boston's Back Bay area, I will never know. The spring rains had hit New England hard, and my windshield wipers were beating futilely against the downpour. With that and my own sobbing, I could barely see the white lines along the road. Besides that, I was shaking with nerves and cold.

Jim could not answer many questions for me, but his kindness and listening ear helped so much. For a long time he sat patiently as I poured out my confusion and hurt. Finally after three hours, when I had gotten myself together, he said, "Why don't you go and talk it out with Frank now?"

He was right, of course. Back to Chestnut Hill I went, driving through the rain and cold darkness. It was not quite eleven P.M. and I knew Frank would be studying in the law school library, so I semi-automatically headed my car toward it.

Inside, I made my way through the stacks and found him at his usual study carrel. Since it was now approaching midnight no one else was around. Frank was relaxing in his chair reading *The Wall Street Journal*. As soon as I laid eyes on him my hurt turned to pure rage.

"Hi, honey," he said, smiling over his paper. "What's new?"

"I've just spent the evening talking to Jim."

"Great," he said absently, glancing back at his paper. "Is everything squared away for this weekend?"

"No, it wasn't so great," I retorted. At once he dropped his paper and looked at me, obviously stunned by the anger he saw on my face.

"Susan, what is it?"

"I just found out that you are a married man!" I shouted.

Frank swallowed hard, his body motionless, the paper frozen in his hands.

After tense moments he let out a sigh and said, "Thank God you know."

"No thanks to you!" I shouted again. Now the floodgates burst open. "How could you have been so dishonest? We've been seeing each other for seven months. We've been talking about marriage. Why didn't you tell me the truth? Don't you think I have a right to know? Everyone knew about this but me!" And then I broke into tears.

Frank stood up beside me. He didn't touch me and it was a good thing, because I might have hit him. He was dumbstruck until I turned on him again. "Aren't you going to say something?"

Quietly, his head hung down, he said, "I always meant to tell you, but . . . well . . . I couldn't right away. It's not something I'm proud of. Then I fell in love with you so fast. And I know how strong your devotion is to the Church. I was afraid that when you found out I'd lose you."

"But I had a right to know," I blurted. "Seven months, Frank. For *seven months* you've let me believe lies. Do you know how that hurts?"

He put his arms around me and I leaned against his chest, sobbing. "Not lies, Susan. Just half-truths," he said miserably.

We left the library and went to an all-night cafeteria. Until nearly three A.M., we talked out our feelings. I listened to Frank's side of the story about the failed marriage and about his hopes that it could be annulled by the Catholic Church. I told him I hoped that could be done, too. Otherwise the Church would still consider him a married man and our relationship would have to end.

As he drove me to my dorm, I leaned my head dejectedly against the window. My mind was numb. When he dropped me off at the curb, I could not kiss him. Curtly, I said, "Good night," then turned my back and went inside.

I was too tired to cry anymore, but lay in the darkness with the enormous pain billowing up inside me. It would be so easy, I thought, if all life's questions had clear black-and-white answers. From my Church training I knew I should refuse to see Frank ever again. But what was I supposed to do with all the love I felt so deeply for him? My head splitting with questions and a near migraine, I forced myself to sleep.

When I awoke the next morning I felt no better. Like a zombie I walked to my early classes, scrawling notes mechanically from the lectures. I had to know what to do about Frank. Catholic annulments were still a rare thing in the '60s, so what should I do?

Just after lunch I had some free time. Walking across the campus, I made my way to the chapel. Since it was midday in the middle of the week the building was deserted. Except for the low light of a few candles, the empty pews were nearly swallowed in darkness. The heat was turned down so it was cold inside, and I drew my coat tightly around me as I slipped into one of the pews. Kneeling, I dropped my head into my hands.

In the stillness my heart cried out to God, laying out all the disappointing facts. I needed God's help to show me what to do. I needed time to think things through. I started talking to God and simply let my feelings spill out as though I were talking to a flesh-and-blood friend.

"Lord, I need Your help. I'm so confused," I whispered. "I don't know what to do. I love Frank so much. But I don't know if I can trust him anymore because of the way he's handled this thing. And I don't want to go against the teaching of the Church. So where does that leave me?"

For well over an hour I knelt there. My emotions rose and fell. At times I was able to hold myself together—and a moment later the tears would come. Perhaps it was not the best time to try to come to a final decision about our relationship, but I persisted. Gradually I felt a sense of peace come over me and all the tension that had knotted itself into a headache seemed to drain away.

Inwardly, words began to form in my head. An inner voice seemed to say, *Continue to support Frank. Stand by him through the struggles ahead. Forgive him for his failings. Your love for him is good.*

Forgive him. That was it. I knelt for some time thanking God for touching me with such a simple answer. More than the answer itself, I was moved by the sense of God's presence and the fact that He—the Creator of the universe—was taking the time to listen to my problems and actually placing a message in my heart. I had never experienced anything quite like that before.

After a while longer I rose and walked out of the dimly lit chapel, squinting in the bright afternoon sunlight. *Forgive him.* It seemed an easy, Christlike solution. I had no idea how difficult it would be to hold onto that inner conviction—not an inkling of the emotional peaks and pits ahead.

Even with my "answer," I found it difficult to face Frank again right away. One part of me still wanted to "ditch" him, while another part wanted desperately to be with him. For the next day or two, I could not even bring myself to return his phone calls. When I finally agreed to see him again, his distress—the unusual rumpled clothes, the sleepless look—made my heart warm toward him at once. It almost made me overlook the fact that he did not apologize. On the other hand, he had some hopeful news.

He had gone to a Catholic priest on campus who suggested that he might hire a canon lawyer and look into having his first marriage annulled. Although the Catholic Church was granting very few annulments in the late 1960s, having listened to Frank's story the priest felt there might be some valid grounds for getting the annulment.

This small upswing of hope was enough to recapture my wavering emotions. At once I pinned all my hopes on Frank's being granted that annulment. Without it, I still felt that we could never marry.

The next two years unfolded bringing with it some major changes in both of our lives. But it did not bring an annulment. After Frank received his law degree in May 1969, he moved to New York City and took a job on Wall Street. One of his dreams was to start his own company and what better place to learn corporate management than in the investment capital of the world? However, I was somewhat surprised at the degree to which his interest in finance ignited into a consuming fascination with corporate power.

In June 1970 I received my Master's degree in Counseling Psychology. I was then faced with the choice of where to move. Frank was elated that I was now free to come to New York. But I had major reservations. Frank had grown so involved with his work that he had made little or no time to pursue the annulment of his first marriage. I felt sure that if I moved to the city as he wanted then there would be little motivation to get the annulment granted. For several months Frank had been putting a lot of pressure on me to marry him outside of the Catholic Church. A common refrain was, "If you really loved me it wouldn't matter where we got married."

I always felt that was unfair. I did love him deeply. But getting married with the blessing of the Church I'd been raised in with my uncle, who was a Jesuit, officiating was very important to me. The struggle of where to move plagued me with a confusion of feelings. I wrestled various scenarios over and over in my head. Finally, I decided to accept a job offer as a counselor at McGill University in Montreal. It would give me an opportunity to live close to my family again before getting married and moving away permanently. But more importantly, it sent the needed message to Frank that I really took our getting married in the eyes of the Church seriously and the sooner he realized that the better for us both.

After a rather difficult showdown weekend when we hassled out what were really the important priorities in our lives Frank admitted that he'd not put much effort into getting the annulment. He promised anew that that would change. Sadly, it seemed to take my move to Montreal to give the needed impetus to something we both said we wanted. I barely restrained myself from saying the thing that had been on my mind for some months: that he seemed to be so caught up in his financial interests that the things of importance to me didn't seem to be so important to him anymore.

During the fall of 1970 I enjoyed being back in Montreal. It was such a cosmopolitan city with a strong international flair. My horse, Gray Dawn, even seemed happy to be back "home" again. When I turned her loose in the old familiar stable yard, she gave her mane a jaunty flip, and I had the feeling that she recognized the place immediately.

When the snow fell in the winter of 1971, Frank and I would meet somewhere in the Adirondack Mountains of New York or in Vermont's Green Mountains for a weekend of skiing. The cold days of flying down the tough runs of Whiteface Mountain or Mount Mansfield were warmed into evenings by a fire with steaming cups of mulled cider. McGill University and New York finance were forgotten then. I loved this man, and I wanted to formalize our life-long commitment to each other. There were moments when the year seemed to drag by interminably.

By the summer of 1971 Frank was getting some informal word that things looked hopeful. Then finally one day in early November I answered my phone to hear Frank's excited announcement: "I've got it! They just called to say the annulment's gone through. Marry me now!"

Though our wedding plans suddenly kicked into high gear, the news was a little anticlimactic after all the struggles we had been through. Nonetheless, my dampened enthusiasm picked up again as Mother and I flung ourselves into planning the gala wedding of my girlhood dreams.

Keeping busy is a great way to avoid life's deeper issues. I would not fully realize that until much later. As Frank and I planned our wedding, writing our own vows and choosing the music, something inside me wanted to raise the question of priorities that had nagged at me periodically during this long wait. But I let it go and funneled my energy into the wedding.

And so, on a gorgeous, clear blue and cold day in February 1972, I stood nervously in the vestibule of the spectacular Ascension Church in Montreal, while the organist began to play that march every little girl dreams of. My hand trembled as I gripped my father's arm and he whispered, "This is it, Susie. Are you ready?"

Everyone had risen to his feet as we stepped through the center doors. My legs felt wobbly, and the beautiful blues, reds, and golds of sunlit stained glass looked shimmery through the traditional veil I had chosen. At the far end of the long aisle stood Frank and his tuxedoed groomsmen opposite my attendants. My uncle was beaming, and I thought I saw him wink—a note of confidence.

The organ thundered as Dad and I moved down the aisle between the forest of well-wishers. Mother was beaming in the front pew when Dad and I stopped alongside Frank. My uncle bade the audience to be seated, then asked the traditional question: "Who gives this young woman to be married?"

"Her mother and I do," answered my father properly, though his voice was thickening with emotion. And then he turned to give me a small kiss before taking his seat beside Mother.

Just before he lifted my veil, I glanced at Frank. Through the shimmering whiteness he looked like someone out of a dream. Someone who was both "Prince Charming" and a stranger at the same time.

Though my heart was thudding with joy, a voice—very small at the back of my thoughts—whispered, *Do you really know this man you are marrying?*

It was a little late to be asking the question.

Immediately following our honeymoon Frank and I set up house in Chicago where a few months before our wedding, Frank's firm had relocated him. He was very sharp at his business, and in a short time had made himself invaluable enough that his bosses quickly decided to give him much more responsibility. To say I was proud would be an understatement. We had found just the right apartment on Lake Shore Drive, just north of downtown. Our apartment was on the twenty-fifth floor, and its southerly panoramic view included Lake Michigan and all of downtown Chicago.

Our honeymoon apartment! At night we would sit and watch the millions of twinkling lights and the living ribbons of traffic flowing up and down Lake Shore Drive far below us. Seeing all those moving lights fed me with an energy from the very pace and beat of the exciting urban life all around me. As soon as the weather turned warmer we played tennis almost nightly at the courts at Irving Park. Life was good and I felt that I had stepped through a magical door into my own fairy tale.

Since it had taken Frank and me nearly three years to get married, I had had a great deal of time to think about what I wanted. I was soon going to be twenty-five, and I had accomplished my Master's degree and gotten some university work under my belt. Frank had a secure, well-paying job. For me, only one thing remained to complete the perfect picture.

It was a warm May evening a little more than three months after our wedding when I decided to take my chances and ask Frank the question that was now in my heart.

Through the open windows, breezes off Lake Michigan blew in the scent of spring—and with it a touch of romance. Frank was due home at any moment. I had fixed his favorite dinner and fussed with the candles and fresh-cut flowers on the table until the setting was perfect. When I heard him coming in the front door, I just had time for a quick glance in the mirror and a moment to smooth my hair. I walked into the parlor as he was setting down his briefcase and loosening his tie. Looking up, his mouth fell open a little. "Wow," he said, grinning.

Seating ourselves at the candlelit table, we clinked our glasses together and laughed. It was a party just for two. And from there the evening unfolded wonderfully. The flowers, the pretty dress, the special meal—I had done it all to show Frank how much I loved him, that I wanted to please him. If the idea I had in mind had not made me a little nervous, I would have been able to enjoy it even more. About halfway through the main course I decided this was the right moment.

"I've been doing some thinking," I said absently, resting my fork against the plate.

"About what?"

"I've been wondering what you'd think about us starting a family."

Frank's fork continued to move mechanically. I thought he was pondering a reply, and waited hopefully. He kept on eating. Hadn't he heard me?

"You know how much I love kids," I pursued, "how I'd love a big family. Maybe even four or five kids. We'd start out with just one, of course." I paused, hoping my attempt at humor would bring a smile. The fork kept moving mechanically.

"This is the perfect age for me to have children, Frank—healthwise, that is. And you'll be thirty pretty soon. Don't you agree that—"

"Susan," Frank interrupted. "I'm not ready for kids."

"Not ready?" The party feeling was starting to fizzle.

"That's what I said. Not ready."

Not tonight, I cautioned myself. But I couldn't help it. "But we waited so long to get married. Can't we at least begin *talking* about starting a family?"

"No." The sharpness of his reply said the issue was closed.

"Why?" I pushed, my voice rising. "Can you explain why you have to be so adamant about it?"

Frank launched into a vehement argument about how important he felt it was to be able to provide properly for his children. He said that if we started a family now it could cramp us financially and there was no way he wanted that for his family. We were only having kids when we had enough money.

My feelings tilted between compassion for Frank's sincere desire to make a better life for his family and my own disappointment.

"Really, Susan," Frank went on, "I just want our kids—and you—to have anything you want. Let's wait until I have my own company. Things will be much more comfortable for us then."

The meal ended quietly—not the comfortable quiet between two people who are eager to spend an evening in each other's arms, but something a little strained. And late that night with Frank asleep beside me, an unspeakable sadness tinged the love I felt for him. My mind replayed the conversation, saying all the things I "should have said."

Just when will we have enough money? How much does "being comfortable" equate to? Are you sure personal finances aren't becoming too high priority for you?

I fell asleep with my head against Frank's, my cheek nestled against his thick hair, wondering if I would ever be able to understand what really went on inside that brilliant mind. He seemed so driven.

My sense of longing and sadness continued for the next week. I had not realized how far apart we were on the issue of children, but I now knew that I was not to push any further. I resolved that I would *not* allow myself to get pregnant until Frank and I were in agreement on the timing. I had known of too many couples who tried to use a baby to plug holes in their marriage only to find themselves in divorce court with a child-custody battle on their hands to boot. And since Frank *was* the other parent, the one who would be saddled with the financial responsibilities during child-rearing years, it would not be fair to him.

4
THE DREAM CRACKS

As the beautiful summer of 1972 unfolded, I decided that it would be best for me to continue my schooling. Since I was not going to be a mother right away, I could take this opportunity to prepare for my future career. I had every intention of devoting myself full-time to my children when they came along, but once they were in school I could reenter the working world. My marketability would be limited with only a Master's degree and so, as fall came around, I began checking into universities in the Chicago area that offered doctoral work in Counseling Psychology.

Throughout the winter I visited campuses and submitted applications. Three of the universities were in the immediate area and two were within weekend commuting distance. The interviews were so thorough, the application procedures so demanding that I sometimes wondered if I would get through *them*, or more importantly, the doctoral studies themselves. After interviewing with many professors, there was little doubt that my first choice for doctoral work was Northwestern University, north of Chicago in Evanston. The faculty that I met during my interview, as well as their intensive program, impressed me far beyond what I had seen anywhere else. So I submitted my application and held my breath.

It was March, not long after Frank and I celebrated our first wedding anniversary, that I stood at our mailbox with an envelope from Northwestern in my hands. I was almost too scared to open it. Then, in a burst of courage, I tore it open, unfolded the single sheet of stationery, and read,

Dear Susan:

We are pleased to inform you that you have been accepted. . . .

I shrieked so loud that I thought our neighbors in the next apartment might call the police. This was the entrance to a whole new path in my lifetime career. Even as I read and reread the brief letter, however, I had no idea just what a difference it *would* make.

When Frank walked in the door that night I was too excited to ask how things were going with the big coal deal he had begun to work on. I had planned to display my letter over dinner but the excitement was obviously bursting through.

"All right," Frank said with a suspicious grin. "What are you smiling about?"

"Oh, nothing," I responded coyly. "I'll tell you about it later."

"Come on," he coaxed, dropping his briefcase into a chair. "What's going on?"

I couldn't stop myself. I began dancing the little jig—our private signal that something fantastic was happening— right in the middle of the living room carpet.

"Susan . . . ? What in heaven's name—"

Still dancing, I pulled the letter out of my back pocket and chirped, "You are looking at the future *Doctor* Susan Stanford Kelly. Northwestern has accepted me!" I finished with a yip of joy and continued my dance.

"Super!" Frank cheered. "Absolutely super. You deserve it."

He went to the wine rack and pulled out a bottle of champagne. I stopped my dance and grew serious. "What if the program turns out to be too much for me?"

Nothing would dampen Frank's determination to celebrate. "Nonsense. You're the brightest and *prettiest* student they'll ever have. I'd say they're doggone lucky." For the next two hours he continued to bolster my ego, telling me how "proud" he was of my intelligence. He was behind me all the way. How I appreciated his support!

The rest of that year brought a whirlwind of changes.

First, of course, I began my postgraduate work in the fall. Daily, I commuted up to the Evanston campus, which is situated along the western shore of Lake Michigan. It was more than three years since I had been in a classroom setting but I was not as rusty at research and writing as I had initially feared.

As it turned out I surprised myself by reaping A's on my very first papers and tests. And I received encouraging attention from my professors. That was all I needed to overcome the needling worry that the studies might be too difficult.

I also began to make new friends. Laura was in most of my classes and I found her a very kind person with a certain sparkle in her eyes. I was drawn to her gentleness. To me, she would make the perfect counselor. I was particularly amazed at her capacity to be interested in other people, even though she was going through a separation with her husband. Though I knew she had hurts, she had an unsinkable manner. I enjoyed the many lunch hours we spent together.

Evenings and weekends I found myself sunk into research at the library or, less often, settled across the living room from Frank as we each worked on our various stacks of reading and papers. We were both so busy that I didn't notice at first how little time we had to talk about our diverging involvements.

Another major change in our lifestyle occurred when Frank and I bought our first home. We had decided it was time to get out of the city and back to the country life we both enjoyed. We purchased a house that included a lovely, secluded piece of property in a town about thirty-five miles north of Chicago.

Situated on a quiet country road, the house was nestled on five acres of land surrounded by thickets of hardwood forest. The long driveway scooped through the woods and swung in front of the house, ending in a four-stall barn. Not only was the setup perfect for keeping horses, but the property abutted picturesque woods and open fields—perfect for long, leisurely rides. Soon after moving into our house, and with Frank's increased interest in riding, we decided to buy another horse, a sturdy mare built for hunting and jumping. Her name was Morning Mist. She was large—sixteen hands high—a beautiful steel gray with a white blaze down her face.

One of my own goals for our buying that house had been that it might become a place where Frank and I could retreat together to simply enjoy each other's company. What with the hectic schedules Frank and I had been keeping, I was excited that we might finally be able to spend some quiet hours together again. I envisioned us riding through a dewy morning woods while summer ripened into fall. The leaves would *scrunch* beneath the horses' hooves. We could stop and picnic and spend tender moments together.

Perhaps I was overly romantic, still in the throes of "honeymooning," but my intended shared time did not last very long.

Rather than draw us together in a mutual interest, the house and horses began to have the opposite effect within just months of our move. Frank's job demanded that he travel and too frequently he was away from home during the week. Somewhat dejected, I found myself eating supper alone by the fireplace on too many evenings. I guess neither of us realized how much responsibility it took to run a household. Besides the normal chores—laundry, cleaning, meals—I had to shoulder everything in Frank's absence. We had decided to board some horses and they added extra work to my already demanding schedule.

It was only a matter of months before a chill began to creep into the house. It was almost imperceptible at first. But then it became more obvious. Frank had been working on the coal deal for months. But it had begun to take him away from me almost every week as he traveled back and forth between states to dicker with the various company owners.

I can't say that I was becoming jealous, but I was beginning to tire of his insatiable drive at the expense of our relationship.

When Frank did arrive home he was often so exhausted he showed little or no interest in what was happening in my life at the university. Too frequently I climbed into bed at night only to find Frank's back turned toward me. Not only did I have to miss him on week nights, but most weekends he was so worn out that he would tumble into bed and be fast asleep in minutes. There he was right next to me, and I was missing him.

The loneliness began to build. And worse than the loneliness was the response he'd developed to my pleas to help share the work load around the house. Early one Saturday we'd gone for an enjoyable ride through the nearby woods. When we returned home I made a list of some of the things that really needed attention around the house. I approached Frank with my list.

"Frank, could you please help me this afternoon with all

the things that need to be done around here? I really need a hand."

"Susan, I hate to do this to you—you know I try to stay away from paperwork on weekends, but I've really got some pressing work that needs my attention."

I was surprised at the degree of resentment as I responded. "*You* go off every week, footloose and fancy-free, while *I* get stuck taking care of everything around here. What about me? What about my schoolwork? Not only do I have to study my brains out—and by the way, my finals are coming up in a couple of weeks—but then I'm supposed to keep up this house and take care of the horses all by myself!"

"I do my share," Frank shot back.

"What?" I challenged. "What do you do besides walk in at the end of the week and expect to be waited on and find clean laundry in your drawers! I'm not your mother."

Frank came on in full attack and was vicious. "If I'd known that getting your doctorate would turn you into a 'women's libber,' I'd never have gone along with it."

" 'Women's libber'? What in heaven's name—?"

"I work pretty doggone hard all week. I come home expecting a little peace and relaxation—and you want to start a fight. I think it comes from all those 'liberated' women you're hanging around with."

"What 'women's lib' stuff? What friends are you talking about? I'm not trying to start a fight. I just want a little help. I can't carry the weight of this place alone."

It was too late to untangle our conversation. I couldn't

make sense of Frank's accusations, and we had smothered the real issues with layers of emotion. Frank disappeared into the house leaving me with both horses to care for.

Later we brewed a pot of tea and tried to make up. Both of us acknowledged that we were pretty threadbare as a result of the hectic schedules we were keeping. Even as we exchanged apologies for the angry words it felt shallow. Like splashing white paint over rotten boards, I allowed Frank to think things were "okay" again when I really felt things needed to change. I just didn't know how to get him to see it from my perspective without winding up in a fight.

The following morning as I dressed for church I approached Frank, who was paging through the newspaper. "Would you like to come to Mass with me this morning?"

Barely glancing up, he replied, "Not this time."

Really, it was a joke. A sad joke. A little game. At first, when Frank would say, "Not this time," we had laughed about it—because it was always, "Not this time." This morning it just hurt.

So I drove to the nearby church all alone. As the young priest said the liturgy, gave his enthusiastic sermon, and invited us to Communion, my thoughts were riveted on one thing. Silently, as I knelt at the altar rail, I prayed: *O God, please help our marriage. It feels like Frank and I are slipping away from each other. We were so in love, and suddenly I'm feeling so alone.*

The next several months found us moving farther and farther apart. It felt to me that Frank cared less and less for those things that were important to me. With little affirmation coming from home I began seeking it more and more at school. Late in the summer of 1974 I allowed the attentions of a physician I knew, who taught at the medical school, to get 'way out of line. My vulnerability left me weak to fight off his over-zealous interest in me. We had a brief affair. But in my heart and because of my faith I knew it was wrong. It was a violation of what I believed marriage still should be.

But in many ways, the fact that I got involved in the affair stunned me into realizing how bad things were with my marriage and my absentee husband. Even my intense loneliness did not justify receiving the attentions of another man or the deception to my husband. I had to face the fact that, except for the months before I discovered Frank's hidden, first marriage, I had been struggling to sense his love for me from the very start. I had accepted superficial evidence—words, promises, dinners out, nice homes—in place of things with true meaning. I wanted his time, attention, emotional support, intimacy. I wanted him to set aside the things that were important to him—not all the time, but at least once in a while—and invest himself in me.

As the winter of 1975 blew in it only reflected on the outside the chill, the emptiness I already felt in my heart. Frank had thrown himself headlong into another "major investment deal." Meanwhile the pressure was really mounting for me. This semester I had to finish up my doctoral dissertation and "defend" its research findings to my doctoral committee. Also I had to prepare for my oral and written comprehensive exams at the end of the semester.

Now I was going to need Frank's support more than I ever had before. Perhaps he would put aside his self-centeredness for a while. My frustration had become ingrained and the distance between us had turned into an ever-present tension. But nothing had matched the fury I felt when that early spring snowstorm hit.

One evening in March I pulled into our driveway just at dusk. The sun, a fiery red, was disappearing behind mountainous, steel-gray clouds. I was exhausted from a full day of classes and term papers in the library. I hadn't even had time to stop for lunch with Laura and a new friend, Dan, who was in one of my classes. The driveway was icy and large snowflakes began drifting between the bare branches. Now and again a slight gust would send the snow eddying like little white imps in a dance.

Frank was home, for a change, and I parked next to his car. A load of books in arm, I slipped along the sidewalk, wishing Frank had spread rock salt on the patches of glare ice, and burst in through the front door. "Honey, I'm home," I called, hanging up my parka.

"Hi," he greeted me, with a kiss. "What's for supper?"

I stiffened a little. "I don't know. I've been at school since eight this morning."

Attempting a joke, Frank patted me on the shoulder. "Give it some thought, will you? Let me know what you come up with."

Grudgingly, I stomped into the kitchen, making sure I banged every pan that I pulled out of the cupboard. Frank was oblivious, but it felt good to vent my irritation. I wanted to sit down and put my feet up, but there was the laundry to do, and then I had a stack of reading. Just rehearsing the mental list made me feel tired.

As we ate, the wind continued to pick up, driving the

snow across the lawns. While I was cleaning up the kitchen, I switched on the radio to keep me company. At first there was a rush of static, then, ". . . high winds, along with heavy accumulations of snow. Chicagoland should pick up about a foot or more by morning, with more snow expected in out-lying areas. . . ."

The announcer continued his weather litany, and I glanced out into the dark backyard. Wind had already curled a huge snowdrift up along the porch. I could not see the trees or the stable through the blinding gusts of snow. Something had to be done about the cars, which were still sitting in the driveway. They would soon be locked in drifts.

"Frank," I said, walking into the living room, "the snow's getting deep outside."

He put down his *Wall Street Journal* and looked at me blankly. "So?"

"*So* if we don't get the cars into the garage they're going to be stuck for sure."

"No, they won't," he murmured, and went back to his reading.

"The radio said we're in for a blizzard. If you help me, it will only take a minute."

"Why do you always make a project out of things, Susan? There's an important story in here that rates this new com-pany I'm after. Can't the cars wait?"

Obviously, he wasn't going to budge. Furious, I pivoted on my heel and went to the front hall. Pulling on boots and my parka, I stepped out into the storm.

Wind was howling through the bare branches. A drift

had risen between the cars and garage, and I attacked it with a shovel. I could see it would take some jockeying to get both cars into the garage, since the driveway was layered with ice beneath the snow. One car was already stuck, and I had to rock it back and forth, stalling in the process, before I could get it to budge. Frank had ignored my request to have snow tires put on the cars, so that made it all the more difficult to get any traction. Twice I had to get out and shovel away the drifts, while more blew in right after it. After a while, the first car was safely in the garage—but there was still no sign of Frank. I had hoped he would check on me when I didn't return right away.

Now I was perspiring inside my parka, though my gloves had soaked through and my hands were freezing. My nose was running, and the sound of my sniffling was competing with the wind. Ice was collecting on the strands of hair that had escaped from under my knitted ski cap. Furious, I attacked the drift surrounding the second car.

One full hour after I had stepped out the door, the two cars were parked in the garage. Frank had not stuck his nose outside—had not even checked on me *once*.

As I slammed the garage door, sadness overtook me. I closed my eyes against the wind and caught my breath. Frank's self-centeredness was suddenly too much. What kind of man had I married? Was this what I could expect for the rest of my life—Frank chasing his millions, while I ran our home like a maid? I supported him in his work. Why couldn't he support me here at home? I was sick of gladhanding words and "I love you." I wanted to *see* that love in action.

When I trudged inside the front door, Frank did not even look up from his paper. I wanted to fall down in the hallway—fake a heart attack—anything that would get him to notice me. Filled with self-pity, I supposed he would merely step over me on his way to the refrigerator.

In the bedroom I stripped off my wet clothes. Finally, too, I was stripping away the small fantasies with which I had adorned our relationship, the pretense that we were a nice, happy, Catholic couple with a rosy future. Why had I refused for so long to see things as they really were?

For a long time I sat beside our bedroom window looking through tears as ice formed on the screens. The reality of what we had—and *didn't* have—as a couple sank in deep. Inside I felt colder than the wet snow that had soaked my skin. Colder than I had ever felt in my whole life.

In that moment in our bedroom I think I gave up. I felt I was facing a granite wall . . . and his name was Frank. Overwhelmed with frustration and loneliness I lay there for a long time and cried and cried.

Frank left early the next morning for work. I got up and, without much forethought, took two suitcases from the closet. Blindly I threw in the first clothes I laid my hands on, then hauled them outside and loaded them in the trunk of my car. My head was pounding as I drove to Laura's apartment. We had become close friends and I hoped I could count on her.

When she answered my knock, she looked surprised and concerned. "Laura," I blurted before she could speak, "I need to stay here. I don't know for how long. Frank and I have been fighting, and I can't go on like this any longer."

Wordlessly, she hugged me. Then she lifted one of the suitcases and said, "You can stay here as long as you need."

Later that morning I phoned Frank at his office. My hands were trembling as the phone rang. As I expected he exploded when I told him I had moved out until we could get ourselves together. "Why don't you get *your* act together?" he yelled. "Straighten up and realize what you're doing. When your dissertation is over you'll see things differently. I can't believe how much you've bought all this 'women's lib' stuff, Susan. You are really overreacting."

We both lost control, saying things we didn't mean. When he paused to catch his breath I shouted into the receiver, "Thanks for nothing!" and slammed it in his ear. Slumped in the chair by the phone I sobbed for a long time.

Though I was immediately distressed at leaving it did not take long for a numbing sense of relief to set in. For one thing, there was not the daily tension, the icy silence to face. Frank would have to hire someone to care for the horses or do it himself. It just might wake him up to all that I'd been handling by myself.

To keep my mind off the disaster at home and to provide some light diversion while bearing down toward the finish line at school, I tried to spend as much time as possible with my closest friends—Laura, Jeanie, and Dan. For weeks Frank and I hardly even spoke by phone. With my friends, however, I could cut loose. We laughed together, talked through final projects, and supported each other without judgment.

In fact, Dan and I were working on a joint presentation for one course so we shared several meals together. He was especially sensitive, listening quietly, directing the conversation with a few well-placed questions. With his natural interest in others he was going to make a great counselor.

One evening in April, just three weeks before my final orals, in which I would defend my dissertation, Dan and I were leaving the library at the same time. "How about stopping at the deli for a bite?" he asked.

I was starving, so I agreed. Over a pastrami sandwich, we talked about my examining committee, and I admitted my fears about facing them.

"Come on," he said teasingly. "You know you'll do okay. You're brilliant, enthusiastic, articulate. How can you miss?"

I chuckled. "Thanks, Dan," I replied. "I don't know what I'd do without you right now."

"Susan," he said, touching my arm, "I'm behind you all the way."

As we left the deli, Dan offered to walk me back to Laura's apartment. As we strode along the quiet streets of Evanston, he slipped his arm over my shoulder. His side was against mine and the touch felt good. Emotionally, I was too exhausted to resist. I allowed the touch—welcomed it.

Falling asleep that night I argued briefly with myself. Getting involved with Dan was *not* going to help iron out problems with Frank. But the months of fighting had taken their toll. I fell asleep with Dan on my mind.

In mid-May I had to face my doctoral committee. Though Frank knew about my exams he never phoned to wish me luck. Walking into the examining room, I wished my husband would have been there to wait outside while I faced one of the most important mornings of my life. But he was not.

For the first half-hour, I answered the committee's questions with a surface calm—careful to keep my sweaty hands hidden under the table. Soon, however, the adrenalin was flowing, and for the next two hours we slipped into a stimulating dialogue. As the session drew to a close, the chairperson reached out her hand to me. "Congratulations, Dr. Susan Stanford Kelly."

When I walked out, my feet were barely touching the ground. I had to find somebody to share this wonderful day with. Perhaps Laura. Rounding a corner, I nearly bumped into Dan. In his hand was a single rose. His eyes met mine and I burst out laughing.

"Doctor?" he offered, grinning.

"Yes!" I shrieked happily. "I passed with flying colors."

That evening Dan treated me to a celebration dinner. Walking into the dimly lit restaurant with him, I pushed Frank out of my mind. He had not even asked if I was all right in the seven weeks since I'd left. *He* should have been there with rose in hand. If he was going to play his self-centered games, then I'd had it.

Dan and I barely touched our food. While soft music played and the candle flickered on our table, I replayed almost word for word the whole two hours of the exam. Dan's eyes hardly left my face. He was so interested, so thrilled for me. When he took my hand across the table, I did not even try to fight the feelings I was having for him. Long after the waiter stopped checking on us, Dan finally said, "Why don't we go somewhere for a drink together, just to cap the night?"

"Great. Where do you suggest?"

"Well," he said, "I *could* suggest my place."

Somewhere inside I heard a distant warning. Sure he was a nice guy. Sure I was feeling good. But what about my marriage? I wasn't listening. He was so close, so warm. Everything in me wanted the beautiful tingling sensation to go on.

"Why not?" I smiled.

I spent the rest of May in Dan's company. Even when Frank returned to Chicago from his business travels, he never bothered to call and see how I was. Meanwhile, Dan and I rode bikes along Lake Michigan, basked in the balmy warmth of spring, and enjoyed each other's company. Our physical involvement continued. The winter had been cold and tough and I almost succeeded in convincing myself I deserved this "fling."

But not quite. When Dan announced that he had plans for the summer that would take him to the West Coast I felt some relief. Guiltily, I thought that maybe I could make a huge effort that coming summer to reconcile with Frank. How was it, I wondered, that beneath all the hurts and anger I loved that man so deeply? Even so, I thought, it would take a miracle to save our relationship.

At least now, I thought, my emotional resources would be stronger. With my studies over I would have time to relax—time to sort out my confusion of guilt, hurt, love, and anger.

Time, however, was the one thing I did not have.

5
THE "PROCEDURE"

June 14, 1975, dawned crisp and clear. Summer weather had not arrived in time for graduation day at Northwestern. After two years of strenuous work and burning the midnight oil, I was finally to receive my Doctoral degree in Counseling Psychology. To my delight the university had even offered me a job as Assistant Professor. How ironic that in acquiring a counseling degree, my private life had run aground. This graduation day should have been one of the happiest in my life—but for the startling discovery I'd made.

About mid-morning I prepared to make the short walk from Laura's apartment to the campus. At a leisurely pace I fixed my hair and got out my dress. Working my arms through the sleeves, I pulled it on—and winced a little. There it was again. For a couple of weeks, I had been experiencing a tenderness in my breasts.

Numbness crept in at the corners of my mind. A week or

so before, a mental tug-of-war had begun. Consciously, I refused to count the number of days since my last period, while my mind called out the tally each morning. I was even more aware than usual of my body. And my monthly cycle was as regular as clockwork—until now, I thought, buttoning the dress.

Gathering up my cap and gown, I stepped out the front door. What a contrast between my growing heaviness and the festive air that seized Evanston. The sun was high in the sky, the streets were lined with cars bearing out-of-state license plates. I fell in step with the stream of pedestrians headed for the campus. Normally, I walked briskly. Today, my feet were like great weights and I was nearly knocked down by a plump woman in a pink suit who marched by me like a bulldog, holding down her matching hat against the stiff breeze.

Somebody's mother, I mused. I had not invited my parents to the graduation ceremonies because I knew I could never face them with my secret. As if I were being dragged to an execution instead of commencement exercises, the crowd was hurrying by me.

Execution. I think I could have faced that rather than the shame and outrage I could imagine on my parents' faces if they found out what their daughter had done. Things like this happened to others. We were a "nice" family. Agony, like a screw, turned and bit into the pit of my stomach. And what about Frank? He would go berserk. Along with these terrifying thoughts the sound of my rhythmic, leaden steps kept a count . . . one . . . two . . . three. . . . How many days was it now? How far developed . . . ?

The "Procedure"

As in a trance, I found my right place in the sea of graduation gowns. Was there a commencement address? I don't recall a word. And then we were standing in rows, moving quickly in long lines up to the podium one by one. No one—not a soul in this crowd or among my friends—knew. I was entirely alone with the secret I bore inside my body. As my name was called, I stepped forward and shook hands with the president of the university. "Congratulations," he said, holding out my diploma.

I smiled woodenly. "Thank you." And I thought, *Yeah, congratulations, Susan. You're pregnant. And the baby's father is not your husband.*

In the week following my graduation I fell into a bleakness. I somehow went through the motions of getting up in the morning and teaching summer school. I barely ate and sleep was fitful. My mind seemed to spin over the same ground again and again until my head ached.

For three years I had wanted a baby so badly—but not this way. There was no question of trying to trick Frank into thinking it was his. I had been away from him for too long, and he was no fool. How much I wanted to go home and dissolve in his arms. Confessing to an affair would have been awful enough—but telling him I was carrying someone else's baby. . . . Even with all the unresolved anger I had toward Frank, I could never do that to him.

The question began to form: What *was* I going to do? I could not consider the options, not at first. And still the mental tug-of-war went on as I felt more changes in my body. How long had it been? Three weeks—four? I was counting, trying to figure how old. . . .

That was the worst part. I could not bring myself to think of the "thing" growing inside my body as a baby. Babies were living beings, with souls, all pink and milky-breathed, with ten little fingers and ten little. . . . Whenever the images began to form, I slammed the lid down on my thoughts and feelings. I could not let myself feel for this—this clump of cells. That's all it was. *Tissue.* That word was neutral, numbing.

At some point—I don't recall when—I felt that this unwanted tissue had to be removed from my body. I would pick up the phone book, find the number of a clinic, and reach for the receiver. Then my hand would freeze.

Waves of agony broke over the walls of numbness. As a Catholic, I had been raised to believe that all life is sacred. Children were considered a blessing from God and a crowning achievement of marriage. Even if I had gotten pregnant outside of marriage that did not give me the right to . . . kill? Murder? What was it I was going to do? *Save my marriage,* I told myself miserably. *This is the only way. You are in a crisis situation, Susan. You've got to do* something.

Even so, my hand came away from the receiver time after time. The indecision unnerved me. My hesitating only made things worse. Nothing would stop that tissue within me from growing, developing. It was like knowing that a malignant tumor was growing inside you and doing nothing about it. Finally I could not stand the pressure. I placed my hand on the phone and the receiver came up with it.

Dialing the clinic I heard the phone ring. I don't know what I had expected but I was relieved that the receptionist's voice was pleasant.

The "Procedure"

"I believe that I'm pregnant," I began awkwardly.

"You *believe* you are? Would you like to come in for a test?"

"No. I *am*," I clarified. "And I'd like to find out about scheduling an appointment to take care of this." I could not get myself to say the word *abortion*. I heard paper rustling as the receptionist flipped through her appointment calendar. I could still hang up.

"The first opening we have is on Tuesday, the first of July. We can get you in at nine. How's that?"

I felt panicky. The first of July was ten days off. Now that I had made my decision I wanted to get this over without delay. I did not want the pregnancy to continue for another day. "Don't you have anything sooner?" I said, my voice quavering.

"I'm so sorry," she continued in her pleasant tone. "We are very busy."

Trying to hide the misery in my voice I finally agreed to take the appointment. When she asked my name, my own would not come out. With as much confidence as I could muster I told her I was Sally Brown.

"Okay, Ms. Brown," she responded, and I could not tell whether she believed me or whether I was the tenth Sally Brown to phone in that week.

I couldn't have cared less if she thought I was lying. Walking into my room I fell on the bed and wept.

For ten more days I talked myself into and out of undergoing "the procedure." Even on the morning of July first, that drizzly, chilly day, I could not rid myself of the tension or look at it as "the best thing, under the circumstances." It was only the fact that I kept slamming the lid down on any escaping emotion that got me into the clinic that morning and gave me the strength to sign "Sally Brown" on the form, in effect asking the doctor to abort my baby.

Except for the moment when the clinic's sympathetic counselor, Julie, asked if I was ready for "the procedure," I had succeeded in subduing all feelings about what I was doing. The fact that I broke then, that I wept like a woman who was losing her soul, should have warned me of the emotional danger I was in. But I could not think beyond the moment, beyond getting "the procedure" over with and getting out of there.

When the nurse came to get me I was dressed in a white hospital gown. Its loose-fitting, shapeless form swallowed me. I might have been anybody, or nobody. Susan or Sally Brown—it hardly mattered. I didn't even care what they did to me from then on.

I glanced at the nurse's face as we walked down the silent corridor. She looked bored, or sullen, evidently not interested in carrying on any conversation. That was fine with me. Still, I could not help feeling that I was suddenly just a number, part of a routine.

She led me into a small room similar to gynecological examining rooms I'd been in during routine checkups in the past. The smell of medical disinfectant was heavy. On one side was a counter with various medical instruments and rolls of gauze. I would not allow my eyes to take in the sight.

"Lie down," the nurse said, not gruffly, but as if I were a child. "The doctor will be with you in a few minutes."

I slid myself onto the narrow bed, which had stirrups at the lower end. For some time I lay there, staring at the ceiling tiles. *Don't think. Don't feel,* I said over and over and over. *Just be strong enough to get through. Hang in there and it'll be over. Be strong.*

In a minute the door opened and I turned my head as the doctor walked in. He was a tall, gray-haired man, probably in his early forties.

"Good day," he began, as if we were going out for coffee. "I'm going to explain the procedure"—there was that disguising term again—"and then I'm going to do it. The whole thing will take approximately twenty minutes or so."

I nodded, not really able to speak for fear I would burst out crying again as I had in Julie's office only fifteen minutes before. He explained that he was going to insert a small tube inside the vagina, through the cervix, and up into the uterus. The tube was attached to a machine that he would then turn on, sucking out the contents of the uterus, removing all cellular growth. "There will be some pain," he acknowledged. "Let me know if it gets to be too much."

Again, I nodded mutely.

Then he proceeded to the lower end of the bed and instructed me to place my feet up in the stirrups. The nurse had come into the room and he mumbled something to her, then turned to me again. "Try to relax," he said, unbelievably. There was no way.

I could feel the tube being inserted, and then a burning sensation that turned at once into intense pain. Throughout my abdomen I was in agony. Clenching my fists and teeth, I determined to bear the pain and not cry out. For some minutes I could hear the doctor moving about. Perspiration collected on my upper lip and forehead.

At last he said, "I'm going to turn on the machine now. In a few minutes, it will all be over."

In a few minutes. Over. Could I hold on that long? There was no backing out now.

The machine was humming suddenly with a dull sucking sound. My abdomen cramped and the pain in my uterus was nearly unbearable. The mechanical whine went on and on. My breath came in shallow, panting gasps, and I thought I would hyperventilate. Biting my lip, I tried to find some spot in a distant corner of my mind where I could hide from the hurt. *Don't think, don't think, don't think. . . .*

When I thought I could not stand the pain and the whine of the machine another moment, the sound stopped. In the silent seconds that followed, something like an electric shock went through me—an overwhelming sense of disbelief at what I had just done. If only I could hold onto the thought that nothing had formed yet. . . .

"That's it," the doctor announced. "It's over."

The nurse asked him something and I barely overheard him say, "Oh, it looks like about six or seven weeks."

I started. Six or seven weeks? I could not tell myself it was impossible that the child we had just aborted was that old. It was *entirely* possible, except I had not expected that. As long as I could think of it as a "lump of cells" it was not quite so awful. Why did I have to overhear his comment?

The doctor was squeezing my arm. "You're fine. You'll be taken to the recovery room to rest for a couple of hours. Then you can go home."

I nodded. Now that my mind was in gear again the torment had begun.

When the doctor left the nurse wheeled me down the hall, her businesslike manner unruffled. My cot was pushed to the designated area, a large room painted an institutional green. Without a word the nurse left me, the squeak of her crepe-soled shoes fading into silence.

Silence. I lay there shaking with my thoughts. *Six or seven weeks.* I had seen textbook pictures of infants *in utero.* At that stage the fetus had already started to take definitive shape—its heart had begun beating and it had fingers and toes. What had I done?

The only thing that prevented that question from erupting in a scream was the arrival of a nurse pushing a cot that bore another patient. The woman was petite with short sandy-blond hair. Her features were sharp, pixy-like. There was something calculated about her. Hard.

As soon as the nurse retreated the woman looked at me and smiled sourly. "No damn roll in the hay is worth this!"

That's for sure, I thought, but could not answer.

No answer was needed. For the next ten minutes she talked nonstop. The air was blue with the profanity spewing out of her mouth. On and on she raved about being more careful with her birth control. She was going to get the guy who had "done this" to her. I wanted to turn away. Get up and run. Anything to escape this wretched tirade.

Finally she addressed one proper English sentence specifically to me. "Is this your first time?"

"Yes," I replied stiffly. I did not want a conversation—not now and certainly not with her.

"Well, it's my fourth," she announced. "And it never gets any better."

Fourth. How could anybody go through *that* four times? Looking at her I felt a surge of pity. While I was torn to the depths of my being, she was hardened.

There was no strength left in me to reach out to her. My doctorate and all my experience in counseling were worthless at that moment. Every bit of energy was focused on surviving what was going on inside of me.

In the next hour-and-a-half my body slowly recovered from the pain and shock of the suction machine. Not so my psyche. The counselor, Julie, had warned me that I might experience a sense of loss. But this was emptiness. Desolation. Or something worse that can never be named. Once I had had a personality, a life, a soul. Now I was a body with broken pieces inside. It was that sense of shattering that I could not get a grip on. Having this foul-mouthed blonde next to me was probably the next-worst thing that could have happened because she seemed to embody the thing that terrified me: She was like a beautiful portrait that had been slashed; someone had tried to mend the canvas, retouch it, but its innate loveliness was gone forever. And now I had been destroyed like that, too.

After another hour the nurse returned to check on me. She said I could get up and go home. I could escape from the blonde now—but not from myself. Dressing, I felt as if I were clothing a plaster mannequin. The arms and legs did not belong to me but to a stranger.

When I walked to the outer room of the clinic I had to

pass Julie's office. She glanced up from a stack of paper-work. "How are you doing, Sally?"

Terrible.

I nodded and kept walking.

I don't know what would have come out if I'd opened my mouth. There was too little left of the real me to speak.

6
DESOLATION

As I awoke on Wednesday morning, the day after the abortion, the sense that I was separated from my inner self, my feelings, was eerie. The sun that bore through my bedroom window touched skin I could not feel. It was warm and light; I was cold and dark. Inwardly there was pain—but that was over there, like an inky substance in a jar on a back shelf of my heart. I could peer into it or ignore it as I chose.

I rose and walked into the bathroom to take my shower. *If I turn the water on scalding hot,* I wondered, *will it burn me?*

Drying myself after the shower, my skin tingled as if my arms and legs were asleep. My shoulder muscles hurt. *Cry. Cry. Cry,* I commanded myself. Nothing would come.

There was something almost disgusting about the fact that I was going through the normal daily routines. Without looking, I reached into my closet for something to wear. Laura greeted me in the kitchen with a cheery smile—a *cau-*

tious, cheery smile. I said words to her, something inanely pat, before leaving to teach one of my classes. As I drove to the campus, I saw people going about their lives as usual and wondered why the world did not just stop spinning. The infinity of my personal tragedy seized me.

Some sense of responsibility forced my legs to carry me into the classroom where students were waiting to receive "great wisdom" from me. The course was "Theories of Counseling." For them I would make myself perform as a professional. *Don't let them see that anything is wrong,* I commanded myself. *Do what you've always done. Everything depends on your keeping the lid on your emotions.*

If the topic I was teaching had been less familiar I'm not sure I would have been able to keep up the masquerade. As it was I knew the material so well I had only to refer to my notes at the beginning of my lecture and then I was off. A second class followed and again I felt like a tape recorder that someone just started and allowed to run.

When I took a break around noon, I retreated to the deli for a sandwich. I didn't have any appetite, but with lunch in hand, I walked to a far edge of campus and sat by the lake. I had to be alone to prepare for the onslaught of more faces, more questions, and one more lecture that day. Why was I forcing myself through this routine? *Because it's your fault you're in this much pain. And you've got to live up to your commitments.*

Mostly, I think, I feared being alone with myself.

Mid-afternoon, I went back to the classroom. The students were assembling as I shuffled my notes. For the third time I began to lecture. Suddenly, nothing was coming without a struggle. I was practically reading the notes. I felt as though I were in an examining room. The faces followed my movements, scrutinized my slightest gesture, read my "body language."

What do you think is wrong with her?

She's not herself.

The mask of flesh was slipping off. Desperation ate at my stomach. From the back of my mind I could hear a scream rising. Making a point in my lecture, I faltered. The notes were a road map of Timbuktu. Useless. Gripping the podium, the floor seemed to be flying up at me. All around were quizzical looks.

O *God, help me.* Immediately, accusation shot down my prayer like a delicate balloon rising. Pray? Now? After what I had done . . . ?

I took a deep breath. The faces, I noticed now, were buried in their notebooks, not studying me at all. No one knew. That relief was the ladder rung I needed to cling to. Some last reserve of emotional strength pushed me up out of the hole and through to the end of the lecture.

I honestly do not know what got me through the next few days. Perhaps the sheer numbness. Perhaps it was that my friends, sensing something was wrong, had surrounded me with care and attention—as much as I'd allow. Laura was warm, motherly but not smothering. And Jeanie seemed to pick up on my distress. Jeanie was an interesting study. There was a deep "presence" about her.

I knew that she was a Christian—in fact, she was a fairly new convert but didn't wear it on her sleeve like some I had seen on college campuses. She never preached, though she never hid her beliefs either. The most striking thing about Jeanie was that she cared about people as people. A warmth radiated from her eyes. She looked at me in a way that said she accepted me, no matter what.

The rest of the week was a lesson in survival. On Friday afternoon, as I drove north out of the city, I felt as though I'd been shoved through an old wringer washer. I had gotten a short call from Frank on Thursday to say he would be away on business over the weekend. His stable help was not available and someone had to care for the horses. After keeping up a mask for students and friends all week the thought of going home to the solitude of summer fields and woods—alone—was a welcome retreat. I could be gone before he returned Sunday and avoid any confrontation about my coming home for good. So I'd agreed to go and take care of the place.

On Saturday morning I rose early, dressed in jeans and a cotton blouse, and went to the stable. It was a sultry July morning. In the stable, the heady, familiar smell of hay and dirt met me. Fleeting thoughts of my girlhood sprang to mind. Simpler days. Yet the memories were bright, not musty with nostalgia. I filled the feed buckets for the horses we were boarding, then moved into Morning Mist's stall. She had become even more special to me since Gray Dawn's death.

She turned her enormous gray head at my greeting and whinnied lightly. A slice of sunlight fell through a crack, igniting the white blaze on her nose. Running my hand along her side, I made my way into the stall until her liquid brown eyes were blinking into mine. She nuzzled my hand, her breath warm against my palm, scenting me for apples or a sugar lump. Suddenly it occurred to me that she had missed me, and the simplicity of her need touched my emptiness. We both needed a ride.

For half the day, Morning Mist and I sauntered through the forested paths and blazing green summer fields near the house. The solid feel of this horse, this living creature, was comfort in itself. And she was more than that—she was friend and silent companion. Only those who deeply love animals know the exchange of comfort that comes in caring for a favorite pet. Being with Morning Mist helped me to touch life again, while inside, the sense of loss shrouded my heart.

At least, I told myself, it was better than sitting in an empty house with my thoughts of Frank. Early in the afternoon, when I led Morning Mist back to her stall, I wondered when I would see Frank again, hoping it would not be until I was a little stronger.

On Sunday I rode again, early, in the wet morning grasses. After I had returned Morning Mist to her stall I went back to the house to clean up. I had just finished tucking my clothes into the suitcase when I heard a noise in the driveway. A car was pulling in—Frank was home early from his trip. There was no escape. I heard him close the front door.

"Susan . . . ?"

My hands were cold and shaking. I had to get out quickly. Avoid any questions. With all the calm I could manage I walked out of the bedroom, leaving my suitcase on the bed, knowing I could not handle a confrontation about why I was not staying. When I greeted him in the kitchen he seemed distracted. If I made polite conversation for a few moments maybe I could slip out without too much of a hassle. Fighting to keep the quaver out of my voice I said, "How was your trip?"

"Okay," he said, fishing in the refrigerator for a bottle of beer.

"That doesn't sound like it was very successful."

"I can't seem to get through to these guys how great this merger would be. It is so frustrating."

"Give them some time, Frank. They may come around to your viewpoint."

He slammed the refrigerator door. "You wouldn't understand." I passed off the insult but the snap in his voice should have been a warning. "It's complicated and the personalities involved are so mixed up."

Unexpectedly, he turned on me. "What about you? Have you come to your senses and decided to move back home?"

It felt like a body punch. I was barely putting one foot in front of the other and struggled to keep my voice even.

"No," I replied quietly. "I think we still need time to solve our problems."

The frustration of his foiled business deal had obviously built to a head. Unfortunately, I was going to be the scapegoat. He hit me with a solid volley. "Well, if you'd get your head straight and realize all you've got here, I'm sure we could work on our problems. I thought you might come to your senses after your dissertation was out of the way but I see that you haven't."

I felt the tension knotting my back muscles again. If only

I'd kept my mouth shut. This conversation was getting explosive. "Until you treat me like I'm more important than this multi-million-dollar career of yours, nothing's going to change. I suggest we see a marriage counselor and begin to mend this marriage."

Frank did not reply, but stalked off to the bedroom to change his clothes. There was no way he could miss my suitcase. When he emerged again his face was drawn tight, and I could see he was ready for a battle.

"Susan, I'm only going to say this one more time. Why don't you get off this stupid trip you're on and start acting like the woman I married?" His voice had risen to a shout. "I'm sick of this garbage. Stop this liberated woman stuff."

What followed was a tirade of yelling and more accusations. His anger battered me. Inwardly, I cried, *Don't do this to me. I can't handle it! Not now.* I could feel the tears rising.

Suddenly, my last bit of strength crumbled. A sob escaped—and tears. My heart was exploding in my chest—not for Frank, or because of his angry attack, but for the child that was lost to me forever.

Burying my face in my hands I sank onto the sofa. A wail rose from my throat, animal pain and mourning combined. Frank's barrage ceased. The crying engulfed me. I cradled myself with aching arms and shook uncontrollably.

Still using brute force, Frank barked, "What are you so worked up about?"

"Leave me alone—*please,*" I begged.

"No. I want to know what's going on with my wife."

Wife, I grimaced inwardly. Between sobs, I choked out a reply. "I haven't lived here in months—but you've been happily occupied with your career. Now just leave me alone."

But he would not. He loomed over me, questioning, demanding. The room was closing in and Frank's inquisition was breaking me down. A taste of stomach bile reached my throat and my face grew hot and moist. "Please," I begged, nearly gagging. "I'm just not well."

"Susan, answer me," he prodded. "What is wrong with you?"

"I'm sick."

"Tell me what you mean."

I was losing ground to the anguish and dizziness. "I've had some—surgery. So please leave me alone. I can't take this right now."

His tone was panicky. "Surgery? What for?"

"Just surgery."

"I have the right to know. Tell me," he demanded.

"Leave me *alone*," I screamed.

"No," he persisted. "What kind of surgery?"

Through streaming tears I looked at him. There was no resistance left. "I've had an *abortion*, Frank. You know what abortion is about, Frank? It's terrible."

Frank stood motionless, gaping at me. Like a scarecrow with the stuffing knocked out, he crumpled into a chair. "No—*No*—*NO!*" Then his eyes shut and tears began to roll down his cheeks.

My breathing was shallow. Panic was rising. There was no way I could handle both of us crying. I had to get out of there. As I rose to leave, however, Frank leaped up. "Don't leave, Susan," he yelled. "I can't stand to be alone right now."

I looked at him miserably. "I just can't handle your emotions. I'm in bad enough shape myself. And besides"—I didn't know if this would bring his fury or more tears—"you weren't the baby's father."

"I don't care," he came back. "Just *please* don't leave."

For some time, we sat at opposite ends of the living room sofa. Whenever a thought pierced the leather covering that had fallen over my mind it was something like this: Here we were, two successful professionals, surrounded by the lovely trappings of our country home—and we were so lost. Our love had not been enough to build the "American dream" life; we were destroying each other.

Like two children we sat and cried. Our pain was so raw that when we spoke at all it was in single words and fragments of thoughts. I thought I would honor Frank's request and stay just for the evening, but I could not stay the night.

Later I drove back to Laura's. If an abyss had opened up in the highway I would gladly have driven my car into it. The muscle tension made my head ache, and I had no idea how I was going to rid myself of these chafing coils of pain that roped themselves around me.

If I had known what Frank was up to almost from the moment I walked out the door, I might have driven my car head-on into a tree. But the things that went on that evening would not burst upon me for some weeks.

The month of August brought little relief. The passage of time did not seem to relieve the intense pain. I survived simply by keeping my exterior mask screwed on tight. All the while, what was left of the inner me was dissolving—the way ice melts over dark winter water. The emotional separation I had felt just after the abortion was becoming unbearable. I was a shriveled soul, hiding in the fog within myself. With horror, I could hear light conversation and comments fall from my lips. Who was that woman out there in the light, keeping up appearances? I no longer knew her. With the passage of each day I seemed to feel more separated from the me I once was.

I went through the motions of living and somehow found myself at the beginning of the fall semester. On the first day of classes I was having lunch with Sue, a woman who had been in some of my classes and still had a year to go toward her doctorate. She and her husband, Jerry, were among the university friends with whom Frank and I had spent time before our separation. Our conversation started lightly enough, with me pretending that my summer had been uneventful.

After a few minutes I noticed that Sue had barely touched her sandwich. Then she cleared her throat nervously, and her tone grew serious. "Susan, I have something to talk to you about."

"What's that?" I answered, thinking it was something to do with school.

"Frank called Jerry last night. They talked for a long time."

Her nervousness infected me. My stomach gripped and my mind was racing.

"Susan, Frank is saying some terrible things about you.

He told Jerry that breaking up was all your fault—that you're sick and have serious psychological problems."

Anger and nausea punched at me. Sue's eyes were filling with tears as she continued. "And he also told Jerry that you've had an affair—and an abortion."

My stomach was retching. *He has no right! How can he broadcast these secrets—things so intimate to me, that I've shared with him in confidence?*

Sue was almost sobbing. Unbelievably, there was more. "I've learned that Jerry and I are not the only ones Frank has called. He claims he's trying to get advice as to what he should do." She paused. "Susan? Susan, are you all right?"

I was shriveling inward, fighting to come back to the surface. My eyes reconnected with hers. As if from a distance, I heard myself say, "I'm devastated."

Sue was a million miles away, her mouth still moving. "You don't have to justify yourself to me. You're my friend, no matter what trouble you're in."

Our lunch was over. Some woman who lived inside my body thanked Sue for offering her friendship. I had to get away from her.

It was that other self—the woman who lived up there on the surface—who taught my classes. The inner me was curled in a dank prison like a grave. It felt as though Frank, in his rampage of revenge, had stripped and killed me—had flung my body out onto the streets to be trampled. If only that body could just stop breathing and moving and talking. Inside I was already at the point of death.

As bad as Sue's revelation was, the worst was yet to come.

For three weeks I avoided friends as much as possible. Their smiles were still in place, their words kinder than before since they knew. That was the thing: They *knew*. The brand, the "scarlet letter" that had been burned onto my soul, was now emblazoned on my body. When we talked my eyes could not meet theirs.

And then in the middle of October it came. I was alone in my office just before three o'clock, with only one lecture class left that Wednesday afternoon. Sunlight skimmed across the desk. The phone rang and I reached for it mechanically, unsuspecting.

It was my mother. "Susan"—the upset tone alarmed me—"I need to talk to you."

Please God, not this. This would be unthinkable. He couldn't have called them. My hands trembled. "Mom, when did you last talk with Frank?"

"Oh . . ." she paused. "About a week ago. We called to wish him a happy birthday." *A week ago. What did he say?* "Susan, I've heard some things about you. I need to ask you some direct questions to find out if they're true or not.

"Is it true you've been involved with someone other than your husband?"

I knew I didn't want to lie. Not to my mom. "Yes. I'm sorry to say that is true."

Instantly, Mother broke down and began sobbing. My own heart was breaking for her. I was a woman of twenty-seven, had left home years ago; Frank had no right to involve my parents and wound them, too. Why, oh why couldn't he have left them out of this misery?

"Mom, I'm so sorry you've been hurt—"

My father's voice interrupted me. I hardly recognized the gruff, angry man at the far end of the line.

"Dad, Frank had no right to drag you into this."

"Susan, I'm only interested in talking about you at the moment. And you had better listen to me."

What followed was a barrage of unbelievable judgment. Raving like a dictator my father exploded with all the pain that Frank's news had brought to my parents.

The receiver was slipping from my hands. For what seemed an eternity, my father's shouting continued to spew from the phone. Was this the same man who had so compassionately helped to save the life of my riding companion, Danielle, when she had had an abortion? I was his own daughter, but there was not a word of compassion for me. Suddenly, I heard a loud click. Dad had slammed the phone in my ear.

Frank had done the unthinkable. He had told my parents. Having gone to them with only his side of the story he had succeeded in isolating my parents from me. My last resort, my own family, was now removed from reach.

I almost could not replace the receiver. Silence swallowed me. When I was able to stand, my legs were shaking.

Walking out of the building, I wandered along the sunlit sidewalks to the edge of Lake Michigan. It was a beautiful blue-sky day. A picture postcard of fall. But I felt as if my life were really over. Frank had succeeded in knocking out every support—my friends, my family. Any shred of dignity was torn away.

I could walk into the water . . . let it close over me. . . .

It was all too much. The woman who was beaten, lying in

prison inside, decided that enough was enough. There were a few responsibilities to tie up. And then. . . .

My glance fell to my wristwatch. Time for my last lecture. Better not stay by this shore alone with the beckoning waters. Not just yet. . . .

But the classroom might have been the bottom of the ocean. I could hardly breathe. My notes were a blur. The lecture I had given several times before washed out of my head. My lower lip was trembling. My back ached.

Spare your class the pitiful sight of a woman's breakdown. I closed my folder. "I'm feeling really under the weather today. Can we cancel? On Monday, we'll pick up where we left off."

There was a scraping of chairs on the tile floor, a shuffling of papers and feet as the room emptied.

Why had I lied to them? For me, there would probably be no Monday.

It was a hope far beyond me just then that, from my darkest prison of despair, I was about to escape into light and a new life.

7
LIFELINES

I'll never know why I agreed to go off for the weekend with a group of five friends from the university. My intentions following the Wednesday phone call from my parents were the bleakest possible. News had come down from the north country that the fall foliage in Wisconsin was the most brilliant and multicolored in years. Perhaps it was to postpone what I felt was inevitable; it also must have been the gentle insistence of Jeanie, Laura, and the others, their exuberance, and the fact that I didn't want to disappoint them. I had no interest in colorful leaves.

Thursday night the six of us convened at one friend's house to be ready for an early departure. When the alarm pierced my fitful sleep at four A.M., I woke from a nightmare in which my father's face loomed over me shouting, and the words were going through me like spears. I could hear the others rustling their way out of the bedclothes, and I dismally rolled out of bed.

We needed an early start to make the ferry out to Rock Island in Lake Michigan where we'd be staying. Jeanie seemed to have been up before us and she called up the stairs excitedly, "Everyone get up and get dressed. The car leaves in twenty minutes."

As we took to the road, knapsacks and sleeping bags heaped in the back of the large station wagon, I slumped despondently in the front seat on the passenger side. Except for the driver and me, everyone else was soon napping again. Our headlights beamed along the dark highway and I stared into the black predawn. I felt my coming was a mistake.

We drove along and an uneasy feeling twisted inside. It was as though my dark prison had been built over a volcano. I felt seismic shakings within, felt agitated and doomed. The station wagon hummed along the highway. My companions slept serenely. I squirmed in my seat. Desperately I hoped that the dawn would bring some relief from the claustrophobic darkness. But as the first gray blushes of sun warmed the eastern horizon there was no relief.

When the sun broke over the land the others woke one by one. Soon we were on the ferry riding the choppy, wind-driven waves. The sky was a cloudless blue. Red, gold, deep crimson adorned the trees on the far shore. The others marveled at the wonder around us. I just stared, gulping in fresh air, hoping to keep down the wild feeling that my flesh was going to split and my wrinkled, dead-leaf soul would blow overboard into the wild waters.

Once we reached the island we drove to a cottage owned

by Jeanie's parents. It was surrounded by tall timbers—
white paper birch, evergreens, and maples of spectacular
reds and golds that seemed to brandish flames. Though I
had always loved the fall, none of this beauty touched me.

That afternoon we explored the island's winding, wooded
paths. The others kept up a cheerful commentary. I was in-
creasingly preoccupied with my inability to maintain bal-
ance. Stones and the roots of trees set an obstacle course.
Then there was the fear of being left alone—that the others
would turn a corner and I would be lost.

Lost. The words fell inside me like a stone clattering down
a bottomless cavern. I was already lost. Mostly, I was preoccupied with death—with how I could end my life.

The sun sank to the horizon and chilly air swirled at our
feet. We retreated to the cabin where someone built a
crackling fire in the fireplace. Laura and Jeanie disappeared
into the kitchen to make supper. Not wanting to talk to anyone I trailed after them.

Jeanie was standing at the stove slicing chunks of meat
into a stewpot. A pile of assorted vegetables lay in a mound
beside her, and at the end of the counter Laura was cutting
up lettuce and tomatoes for a salad.

"Can I help?" I asked dully.

"I think everything's under control," Laura replied.
"We'll be eating soon and. . . ." Her words seemed to trail
off as my eyes lighted upon the utensil drawer that hung
open. In one slot was a group of chopping knives. Laura
continued talking and all I could do was stare at the bright
blades with a sickening image before my eyes.

"Susan?"

I looked up embarrassed to see that both Laura and Jeanie were watching me. "Is something wrong?" Jeanie probed delicately. "You've been distracted for days."

"No. I'm okay," I mumbled. My tone betrayed the lie.

"We're your friends," Jeanie pursued. "You can talk to us."

"Thanks," I replied. "I just don't want to burden you. You've all come to get away from the books and you don't need to hear any more about the mess of my life."

"Come on. We're willing to listen—any time you're ready."

I nodded. "Sure."

As we sat around the fire, steaming plates of stew balanced on our knees, I thought I was going to start climbing the walls. Flames leaped from the wood. Laughter and friendly talk surrounded me. The others ate ravenously while my food mostly went untouched. Nothing in this idyllic scene held any joy or hope for me. I had to get out.

After supper Jeanie got out her guitar. In her rich, mellow voice, she began singing. Staring into the fire, I could see those knives in the kitchen drawer. *Tomorrow. When they go out hiking again, I'll tell them I need a nap.* Yes, tomorrow. But for the moment when the blade met my wrists, that would end the unceasing torment of my pain.

My friends were into their sing-along now with their feet tapping and hands lightly clapping. I was an outsider. In between songs I got up and said, to no one in particular, "I'm kind of tired—and my back is very stiff. Guess I'll go up to bed." Jeanie and Laura were aware that I had been having trouble with my back so it was a plausible excuse.

Someone else was suggesting that they make cocoa. Jeanie set her guitar aside and said, "Let me come and give you a backrub, Susan. Okay?"

I shrugged.

Upstairs, I sprawled on top of my sleeping bag. Jeanie came in, knelt down beside me on the floor, and started to knead the painful knots around my lower and middle back.

"Susan," she said, a little timidly, "would you mind if I said a prayer for you?"

I was surprised. Accusations ricocheted inside me. *Don't you know, Jeanie? I'm lower than dirt. What God would listen to a prayer for a sinner like me?* But I replied, "Sure, if you want."

Clearing her throat as her hands continued to knead, Jeanie started to speak in a soft voice.

"Dear Jesus, I'm not sure of what to say. But I come to You in prayer for my friend Susan."

As I lay there listening I was amazed at the simplicity of her words. Even more amazing was her childlike confidence that God was actually listening to her prayers. Only once had I really known that He'd heard and answered me—the time I discovered Frank's secret about his first marriage and felt that God wanted me to forgive him. Jeanie's prayer went on for five or ten minutes, interspersed with times of silence while she continually rubbed my back. There was such gentleness, depth of spirit.

As I grew drowsy I heard her conclude: "Susan is hurting badly, Lord. Reach down and touch her. Let her know that *You* are the solution. Let her not despair. She is my good friend, and I care about her so much. I know that You are the Almighty. You can do all things. And You can help her."

Then she leaned forward, gave me a hug, and said goodnight. Switching off the light, she quietly slipped from the room.

Groggily, I worked out of my clothes and into the sleeping bag. My mind drifted from thought to thought. *How lucky to have a friend like Jeanie. Ironic that she should pray for someone like me—thinking I was merely troubled about my disintegrating marriage. Poor thing. She didn't know that God could not possibly hear her prayers for me, a woman who aborted her baby. Too bad her help had to come so late. . . .*

The very next thing I knew was the touch of early morning sunlight streaming through the window. I awoke feeling that I had been sleeping in a pool of warmth and brightness. My first thoughts were of Jeanie and her prayer.

No one else was stirring. I crawled out of my sleeping bag, noticing that the pain in my back was gone. I stepped into my blue jeans, pulled on my big Icelandic sweater, and walked outside into the cool mists of morning.

At the water's edge, I sat on a large outcropping of rock. The air was unmoving, the surface of the lake serene. In the stillness I heard the delicate *whirr* of birds' wings in the branches above me. Only distantly was I aware that I felt incredibly rested, that I must have passed the night in deep sleep.

When—after a long and indefinite time—my stomach began to growl I imagined that someone in the cabin must be up. I could get coffee brewing for everyone and start breakfast. I started up the path to the cabin. Halfway, I caught my breath.

Before me was a stand of tall tapering evergreens directing my gaze upward into the vault of cobalt sky. The enormity of this beauty had seized me unaware. Only yesterday I'd been incapable of tasting this wonder. Now it seemed that every pore was open.

As I continued my walk up the path I would not have described myself as yet "alive." It was just such a marvel that the numbness was gone—that I was not inwardly dead. Though I was nowhere near free from pain and guilt, it was as though the walls of my prison had been bashed through allowing freshness to wash away stale air. I was not quite ready to acknowledge that perhaps God had answered Jeanie's prayer. That possibility still seemed remote. But I realized I wasn't consumed with the conclusion that the only way to end my pain was to end my life.

Opening the screen door of the cottage I heard voices in the kitchen. Everyone was up, planning the day's adventures around the noisily perking coffeepot. How good it was to see their faces turn to greet me.

"Good morning," I said. "The lake is absolutely beautiful."

"So you think it's going to be a good day?" Jeanie prompted.

When we could step away by ourselves, I said, "It's strange. But I feel somewhat better this morning. All the *facts* are still the same. But something's different in me. I don't feel the despair I felt last night. Things don't seem so impossible anymore. Thanks for caring."

Jeanie had been watching intently. "I felt so—inadequate last night, but it was like I was *drawn* with a sort of inner tugging to pray for you. I've never prayed for anyone out loud before but I knew I had to.

"And do you know," she said, "I felt that we were not alone. I knew I had to talk to God for you because you couldn't. Actually, I sort of hoped you had fallen asleep," she smiled sheepishly.

"Your prayer was wonderful," I replied, squeezing her arm. I could not tell her I had been on the verge of suicide. "You'll never know how important it was to me."

The rest of the day was uneventful but for the fact that I enjoyed myself. On Sunday we returned to Evanston.

In the coming weeks, I continued to wobble along between relief and self-hatred. At least I was able to teach my classes and meet my professional obligations. Then in late November another very interesting friend found her way into my life.

Maria was married to Jack, one of the students in our Master's program. I met her at a party in their home—which Jack had insisted I attend. Though I was not up to partying, I went home that night strangely warmed by the conversation Maria and I had had.

For one thing I learned that Jack, who was in his early forties, had decided to get out of investment banking and into counseling after their marriage had nearly fallen apart. Counseling had made a tremendous difference for them and, after emerging from the process, both Jack and Maria were enthusiastic about helping others. She was also thinking about going back to school and I agreed to meet with her to discuss her options.

But more than that there was a warmth about Maria that drew me to her—something bright and wonderful. It was the same brightness that I felt in Jeanie's presence.

When Maria arrived in my office the week after the party, her cheeks were pink with the nip of early December air and her excitement. She greeted me as if we were old friends. "This is wonderful. I can't believe I'm going back to school after all these years. Jack is thrilled for me."

The remark stung. Frank's exuberance for my going back to school had never gone beyond the bottle of champagne we opened on the day I was accepted at Northwestern. And it hurt to be with someone who had saved her marriage when mine was obviously over.

"Whatever drew you to counseling in the first place?" I asked, with more than academic interest. I really knew very little about Jack and Maria, except for the broad reference to past marital problems he had made at the party. From Maria I learned that five years before their differences had been so bad, the situation so hopeless, that they had filed papers for a divorce.

"Then I found myself reaching out for a faith that had died years ago," Maria explained. She had my interest. "First, God seemed to open my eyes and I saw our situation in a new light. I told Him I'd give the marriage one more try. Jack agreed to go to a marriage counselor"—my spirits, which had been rising, dropped again—"and we learned how to really listen to each other. With God's help, we were able to forgive one another and let go of the past."

Maria's referring to God so personally, the way Jeanie had, her candor and peace all gave me hope. There was nothing "holier-than-thou." Nothing put on.

I wondered if God was trying to tell me something through these two marvelous friends. Did He have a message for me?

Immediately I dismissed the notion. I had gone against everything I'd been brought up to believe. Nothing in me said that my sin could be forgiven. To me, I was detestable. Abortion meant excommunication.

When we finished our conversation we agreed to meet again to talk more. It was three weeks after that, just before Christmas, that we were seated in the campus deli. Just as the waitress set our meals before us Maria asked, "Do you mind if I say grace?"

"Why—no," I replied, somewhat surprised. Lightly, she took my hand. Her prayer was simple and short, and when she looked up again I said, "Your faith is really important to you, isn't it?"

"Yes. It's become the center of my life, in fact. I love Jack and the children very much, but my family would be in total shambles now if it weren't for the way the Lord healed our fractured relationships."

I set my sandwich aside and commented absently, "It's nice that you feel God was such an important help in saving your marriage."

She stopped in mid-bite. "Oh, no. He wasn't just an important help—*He* was the crucial element that saved it!"

"What about counseling? You said that was important, too."

"Of course. But we never would have gotten to the counseling stage if it hadn't been for what God did for me before that."

I looked at her questioningly.

"Susan, Jesus taught me what it means to be truly forgiven. I told you several weeks ago that our marriage had been in terrible shape. That was an understatement. I had been involved in an affair—and I mean really involved. Long-term. I never thought I could give it up."

I hoped I wasn't flushing. Since it seemed imminent that my marriage was going to end in divorce the thought had crossed my mind that I might still turn to Dan. Even though after the abortion I had written and told him I could not see him again, I wondered selfishly if he could help the loneliness I still felt.

Maria had not noticed that I was so startled I had stopped eating. "I felt so terrible for the duplicity," she was saying. "I was sure I could never get my life together again. But I knew that even if my marriage never came together, I had to let go of that affair.

"And that's where God came in. He gave me the strength and determination to get out of it. Most important, He showed me I could be forgiven—and that I had to forgive myself for the lies and cheating. For the first time I understood why Jesus died on the Cross—for my sins, Susan. And for yours."

She was speaking in general but I almost winced because

I knew my own deep-down specifics. Maria went on for a few minutes more saying that she had been a "nominal Christian"—a category I was sure I fell into as well—that there were things she deeply regretted, but that Jesus had set her free from her old life by His death and resurrection. Eventually, Jack came to develop a faith in God, and from there their lives were rebuilt.

Lunch was over and we had bundled out into the chilly December afternoon. I said, as we parted company, "I'd like to get together again sometime, Maria—if you're willing. This was extremely helpful. Maybe I can learn a lot from you."

About three days before Christmas, my father phoned. It was the first time we had spoken in more than two months. Stiffly, he asked if I planned to come home for the holidays. There was no apology. In fact, no reference at all to the last time we'd talked.

Even so, as soon as I heard his voice, everything in me cried out for *home*. How I wanted to be with my mother and father—to be surrounded with love, since I was still so full of self-hatred. Yes, I said, I would be home for Christmas.

It was a quiet disaster. None of the colored lights or glittering tinsel could cover up the tight-lipped silence that hung between us. There was the usual scent of evergreen, pretty paper, and bows—and nothing but disappointment within me. *I have done this*, an inner voice accused. I had not only shattered my own life, but had wounded everyone around me.

When I returned to Evanston shortly after New Year's, I sincerely hoped that 1976 would be a better year than the one before. Cynically, I decided it could not possibly be any worse.

Though I was beyond thoughts of suicide, I wasn't sure that things were really any better in the long run. My private death wish had passed back in October at Rock Island, but I wasn't too far beyond that emotionally. There was no real life or hope in me. Each gray winter day blended into another. Being at home for Christmas had actually been worse, because it reminded me of the Susan I had been. Exuberant. Full of joy. Outgoing. That Susan lay dead on a table in an abortion clinic. I had killed *her* there as well.

January slipped into February and I could not shake the darkness that covered my spirit. If the wall of my prison had been broken through on that serene morning at the shore of Lake Michigan, I had yet to find a way to step through it. I met Maria for lunch several times and listened to her talk about her personal relationship with Jesus. Jeanie seemed to know Him like that, too, but that was a foreign language to me. Others might find a way out of the darkness in their lives, but me . . . ? I doubted I would ever be able to bask in that kind of forgiveness.

Then one nondescript rainy day in late February, Jeanie asked if she could talk to me after a class. We walked back to my office and as I set my notes down, she announced, "I have a gift for you."

She reached into her purse and pulled out a cassette tape. "I think you'll enjoy listening to this tape of Father John Powell. He's a Jesuit priest who is a popular author and lecturer."

"What's it about?"

"Oh," she replied vaguely, "it's about God's love—it's very good, really—and forgiveness."

I thanked her and took it, promising to listen to it over the weekend. I had no idea how pivotal that innocent-looking tape was going to be in my life.

That weekend I decided to keep to myself because I needed space and time to be alone. In late fall, I had moved Morning Mist to a boarding stable about fifteen minutes from my apartment in Evanston. On Saturday and Sunday both I visited her, and enjoyed two pleasant days with this magnificent animal that meant so much to me. I always believed that some animals have a special sensitivity to their owners, an instinct that tells them when someone is hurting. Morning Mist was gentle, nuzzling me as I brushed her down. She was a real friend and companion.

Returning to my apartment Sunday evening, I suddenly remembered the tape. I popped it into the cassette player and began to fix supper. Father Powell's voice was deep and very soothing. There was a calmness in his words as he spoke about God's love for each of us. At first, it was like listening to someone speak on the subject of astronomy—light-years beyond me.

I let the tape run throughout my solitary meal. The words rolled over me, making little impression. But at some point—I don't know why—I decided that I ought to be open to hearing about God's love. *If* God really loved me, as this man said, I ought to give it a chance. But what if I reached out for this love and it wasn't there? What if I was beyond His love?

For the duration of the message—a full ninety minutes—I

simply held myself open. I could not risk reaching my hand out through the hole in my prison wall.

I was placing my dishes in the sink when Father Powell concluded his message. Walking toward the tape player, I was about to switch it off. As I moved my finger to the button, I hesitated. *Is God's love real—or isn't it?* For several months, Jeanie and Maria had been telling me about this wonderful discovery they had made—the forgiving love of a heavenly Father. Could it possibly be there for me, too?

Without any real conscious decision something inside me decided to ask for myself. Leaving the dirty dishes and tape recorder behind in the kitchen, I quietly walked into my bedroom and got down on my knees beside my bed for the first time in a very long while.

"God, I don't know how to begin this . . . but I can't go on with this emptiness, this desolation. My friends talk of You so personally. They tell me that You forgive all our sins. Do I dare to ask? I wish You could forgive me, too, Lord. I am sorry. So sorry for aborting my baby. . . ."

The tears were flowing and I kept on. "God, I'm so, so sorry. I never meant to make such a mess of my life. But this is where I am now. I can no longer carry all this pain and guilt and heaviness and self-hatred. Can You help me? Please? I don't know what else to say, and words surely aren't enough. But if You can forgive me . . . I'm so sick of all this pain and I'm sorry for all I've done."

With that my head fell forward on the bed and sobbing took control of my whole being. Tears burned my eyes and I shook violently. On and on it went, as a wail of grief rose from the depths of me. Months of torment, fear, confusion

gathered in that wail and escaped from my being. For two hours I knelt there, alternately sobbing and praying, handing my pain to God, for it was too much for me to try to carry any longer.

Some time after eleven P.M., the tears ceased. I was emptied at last. Not like the fearsome hollowness I had felt for so long, but clean. Like a filthy prison that has been opened to the air and scoured of its contagion. When I stood, it was almost as if strong arms raised me to my feet.

Not that I had heavenly visions. I did not. My mind was blank but for the desire for simple things. I took a shower. Dried my hair. Brushed my teeth. Went to bed. I was totally spent and had emptied all my feelings to God.

Monday morning I awoke early as usual. Even before my eyes were clear I knew something was different. It was the strangest sensation, so unfamiliar. I felt *light*. Rolling out of bed, I stood, feeling that I was drifting three feet off the ground. I was like a helium balloon kept in a box, and now the lid was off. I was so taken with the feeling itself, I could not imagine what was going on.

It was twenty minutes later, as I was stepping into my camel skirt, that I paused with one foot in the air. *The hatred is gone—and the pain. It can't be. . . .* I was already heading for the phone, nearly tripping, still pulling on the skirt. *I can't really be free, can I?*

I dialed Maria's number. One ring. Gone was the inner blackness. Gone was the guilt. Two rings. Maria answered, "Hello?"

"This is Susan," I nearly shouted into the phone. "Something amazing has happened."

"What?" she replied, picking up on my excitement.

"I don't know. I can't understand it all. I listened to a tape Jeanie gave me—on forgiveness. Then I got down on my knees and prayed. I know this doesn't make sense, but this morning I'm a different person. My whole being feels light as air and all my self-hatred has gone. This doesn't fit into any of my counseling theories. People don't just *get healed* like that!"

"Oh, yes, they do," Maria crowed. I could tell she was smiling ear-to-ear.

"Well, if that's true, it's a miracle," I said incredulously.

"Yes—exactly!"

We agreed to meet for lunch in two days, our first opportunity.

During those two days I searched within myself for signs that the miracle was crumbling, that the light of glory was fading, or the heaviness crushing in again. But the lightness and peace continued. This was no fragile, ethereal experience. It was *real* at the core of my soul. And it was blowing my mind because I had never read about anything like this in any of my psychology textbooks. Where had all these counselors missed the boat?

When Maria and I met, we threw our arms around each other. We were no longer just friends—somehow we were sisters. The wall that had separated me from my own feelings had also kept me isolated from people for months. Now it was destroyed.

Over lunch I recounted every detail of what had happened. Maria could not stop smiling or remarking how radiant my face was. The healing I had received on Sunday was still real to me—strangely, more real than even the chrome and plastic chair I was sitting on.

This was the new beginning I had not thought possible. Now I felt ready for life again, ready for anything that might be thrown at me. Unbelievably, I knew I had God on my side with His arms securely around me. It was all so fantastic that it hardly seemed real. Yet I was truly happier than I'd been in months . . . in years! With God's help I had hope and felt I could handle whatever came my way. I was going to need it for the times just ahead.

8
LEARNING
TO TRUST

Spring warmed Evanston. Maria and I met once a week to read the Bible and pray. My desire to learn about this wonderful heavenly Father was insatiable. I began a daily private devotional time with the Lord. It became a beautiful sharing communion in which I thanked God for my healing. I wanted a new and deep relationship with Him. For the first time in more than two years I felt totally whole and free from guilt.

It was a new beginning and I wondered what lay ahead. How good it felt to bask in the joy and freedom my healing had brought. Yet I was to learn that the Christian life was not lived on a one-time, other-worldly experience. A season of tough growth was just ahead.

As summer blossomed I developed a strong desire to dedicate my life and work to God. How marvelous if, in some way, I and my counseling abilities could be used to heal others. I sensed immediately that He wanted me to walk closely with Him, to develop spiritual strength through listening quietly for His voice. Again and again I asked Him to guide me through my first tentative steps on this new journey.

I'm not sure I would have asked so eagerly that God unfold His will, had I known what that would cost!

There were many lessons for me to learn regarding my Christian walk. One of the important ones was in the area of material possessions. When it finally became clear in the spring of 1976 that there was no way to salvage our marriage, Frank and I met several times to try and work out a division of our joint property.

I was stunned by what seemed to me a ruthlessness in Frank I'd never seen to this degree. It felt to me as if he was determined that I was going to "pay" for all that I had done. While we were able to come to an agreement on most of our household goods, the bigger ticket items like our home, horses, joint checking account, and bank loans were another matter altogether.

Frank verbally threatened to make it "very sticky" for me if I did not agree to the financial settlement he wanted—that is, he would tell the judge all about my affair, pregnancy, and abortion if I did not agree to sign over most of the big items to him. Based on past experience I knew this was not an idle threat.

I was shaken. At first I was afraid of Frank's callousness, scared that I would be turned away with nothing. Yet the underlying peace never left. Each time I prayed I sensed an inner nudge from God, and the words: *Trust Me. I'll take care of you. Don't trust in worldly things. Trust in Me.*

And it seemed that I kept stumbling across the Scripture in Luke, chapter twelve, where Jesus said, "Don't worry about the food you need to stay alive, or about the clothes you need for your body. . . . Your Father knows you need these things. Instead be concerned with His Kingdom, and He will provide what you need."

Don't worry. I rolled the words over in my head. *Be concerned with His Kingdom.* Did that mean He had some specific work for me to do in His service? What with a whirlwind of legalities facing me just then, I did not have much time to consider what that work might be.

This totally trusting in God for my well-being was new for me. It was so opposite to what the world teaches. But the more I prayed the more the Lord convinced me that I was to rely on Him. If I was going to walk His walk and do His will, then the sooner I learned to follow His lead the better.

So I found myself put out on the doorstep with very little money, the clothes on my back, and my old, dear friend, Morning Mist. She had become even more important to me since the final separation from Frank. For weeks I wrestled with the grief of divorce—it had always been something I felt happened to other people. But in no way was I going to shoulder the full responsibility for it, now that I saw clearly that Frank had never loved me as much as his millionaire career fantasies. In part, though, the divorce *was* an evil fruit produced by my having had an affair. And I had to accept my responsibility for that.

Surely, I thought, *the consequences are over now.* And when I continued to pray, the answer came: *Frank is determined to do it his way. Leave him to Me, now. I know what I am doing with your life. I want you to live it My way. Trust Me.*

I could have allowed anger and bitterness at the terrible inequity of our financial settlement to ruin me. But I decided to take God's view of the situation. Now that most of my worldly connections to the past were wiped away, perhaps I could start from ground zero and rebuild my new life. God and I were going to begin afresh. But how blind I was to the things that still bound me to my past life.

The summer of my abortion Dan had finished his own degree and accepted a job on the West Coast. While our contact during the year since his move had been minimal, in some small way I was still tied to him emotionally. For his part the tie was much stronger. He had periodically written me and would share at some length how much he felt he still loved me. Initially, I had discouraged all his requests for us to meet for a long weekend. But once it was clear that my marriage was ending in divorce I had allowed my thoughts and feelings to turn toward Dan. His persistence paid off and I agreed to meet him one weekend after the divorce was final. After more than a year since I'd seen him, I was curious as to how I would feel.

He was still the caring, sensitive Dan I had known. Tenderly, he would take my hand, walk by my side, and listen to whatever was on my mind. For some reason I found it difficult to talk to him about my newfound faith. It seemed so hypocritical to be talking as if I had become Joan of Arc when I had had an adulterous affair with him. So Christ was pushed to the side of our renewed relationship and I could not help receiving Dan's gentle touch. How I needed a warm, sensitive man just then.

But every time I was with him, there was an odd, troubled feeling within. I might have taken Dan's being there for me as a perfect piece of the puzzle: my marriage dissolves, and this caring man is waiting for me with open arms. But the affair and subsequent abortion were the worst things I'd been through in my life, and Dan had certainly played a role. I was attracted to the beautiful person he was, and felt torn between ending the relationship and allowing it to take its course.

Asking God for guidance was something of a pretense. In some ways I didn't want to hear what God had to say. The strong impression I felt was that the relationship was not in His will for me. But as Dan steadfastly pressed me to see him frequently, I did not have the guts to turn him away entirely, though we did not become involved again physically. Still my feelings and my emotional needs began to sway me from following God's inner nudge.

Nor did my move to Michigan help much. Earlier in the fall I had accepted a job offer from Wayne State University in Detroit. It did not take me long to find a quiet little country place with a small stable for Morning Mist.

First, there was the loneliness. Maria and Jeanie were now several hours away in Evanston. When I returned from Wayne State each evening the phone never rang, since I had made no friends in that area yet. More and more, I looked forward to Dan's phone calls and letters. He once again began to fill an incredible void.

In November, only weeks after moving into the country house outside Detroit, God again moved dramatically in my life.

One night, I was startled out of a sound sleep by a loud banging. Bleary-eyed, I glanced at the bedside clock. Three-fifteen. What was going on ... ? There was the banging again, somewhere out in the yard.

Pulling on jeans and a parka, I stepped out into the frosty air. There was no moon and the night was black. Cautiously, I peered about as the cool of the earth seeped through my shoes. Again I heard the banging, and knew at once it was coming from behind the barn. I ran the distance from the back door to the barn where I saw that Morning Mist was not in her stall. At once I was concerned because I had bred her in the spring and she was in foal. Around the barn I went, half-stumbling. There in the dark I could barely make out the gray figure lying on the ground next to the rail fence.

When I approached Morning Mist I knew immediately that something was dreadfully wrong. She was down and occasionally she rolled from side to side as if she were delirious with fever and pain. She was soaking wet.

I had to prevent her from breaking a leg in her wild thrashing, and somehow forced her to her feet. She was shivering in the November night air, so I half-led, half-dragged her back to her stall. Her eyes were glazed, and she did not nuzzle me as usual when I dried her and covered her with a horse blanket.

My heart pounding, I sprinted back to the house. The

crashing feeling of loneliness was awful. I had begun praying the moment I found Morning Mist in distress, and as I
reached the back door, I focused my prayers on finding
help. Something was terribly wrong, and I feared that she
might catch pneumonia as an added complication. *Father, I
don't even know a vet in this area. And it's quarter to four in the
morning.*

Grabbing the phone book, I chose the first veterinarian
listed and dialed with shaking hands. The fact that I was a
newcomer and not a "regular" was underscored by the vet's
answering service. Did I know it was the middle of the night
and Dr. Hall was home asleep? I begged her to ring him
anyway. Then I put down the receiver to wait.

In a moment, the phone rang. Snatching it up, I was
greeted by a groggy-sounding male voice. Was this *really* an
emergency? I apologized profusely for calling at this hour.
But when I described Morning Mist's behavior, he came to
life at once and took directions to my place.

When we hung up I headed out to the barn again. Under
the glaring light of a bare bulb Morning Mist looked miserable. Her forelock was matted with sweat and her head
hung despondently. *Please, Lord,* I prayed, *please, Lord. No
more loss. She's all I have left. She's like my best friend. If I have to
lose anything take the foal, but spare Morning Mist.*

In twenty minutes Dr. Hall arrived and checked her vital
signs. When he did a pelvic examination, he announced,
"Something doesn't feel quite right. This foal feels very
small. As far along as she is, something's wrong."

He also gave the distressing news that her temperature

was soaring. She had developed a bad colic, similar to flu in humans. He gave her a shot to combat the fever and worried out loud about pneumonia and the life of the foal.

"There's no chance I'm going to lose her, is there?"

The fact that he did not give me a clear answer upset me greatly. He told me to keep in touch and said that he would consider himself on call for me and my mare.

Dawn was too slow in coming. I had remained with the horse I loved but she continued to get worse, sometimes standing listlessly for hours and other times bumping into the walls in a daze. I could not get her to eat or drink. She was becoming dehydrated. Tears ran down my cheeks.

As the morning light grew to full day I returned to the house but checked on her every twenty minutes or so. Around noon I phoned Dr. Hall again. "There's no change," I reported.

"Nothing at all? I can't understand it. I gave her a large dosage."

Later, he came to examine her again. The news was very bad. "She's developed pneumonia," he said, shaking his head.

I was frayed from lack of sleep and did not want to hear this.

He promised that if she did not respond to the drugs by the following morning, he would take her to his clinic. He left, muttering, "Just don't understand it. Something's not right with that foal."

I phoned the university and had my secretary cancel the afternoon appointments with several students. Fortunately, I had no classes to teach that day. When I hung up, sorrow and loneliness blanketed me. *Lord, why aren't You answering my prayers? Why won't You heal Morning Mist? What is it You want of me?*

For hours I tried to distract myself with some reading. Not a chance. My mind never left that stall, and every twenty minutes I looked in on my mare. If anything, she seemed worse. In the evening, I checked in with Dr. Hall, who encouraged me to phone any time I needed him. Exhausted, I set my alarm and collapsed on the sofa.

At two A.M., the alarm jarred me from my sleep. I got up and found my way out through the darkness. Before I reached the barn, I heard the terrible thrashing.

Running inside the barn, I shrieked in horror and dismay. Morning Mist was throwing herself against the sides of her stall. In her delirium, she had struck one eye on a nail sticking out of the wall, and red streaks of blood covered the white blaze on her face.

I nearly vomited. "O God, no . . ." I moaned, "she's all I have left in the world. . . . Please, God. . . ."

When my legs would hold me, I rushed up to the house to call Dr. Hall.

"I'll be right there," he replied grimly, when I told him the situation. "And stay out of that stall! She could trample you without knowing what she's doing."

I hung up and, not knowing what else to do, collapsed on my knees. After two nights without much sleep, I was coming unglued emotionally. Choking on my tears, I prayed, "Lord Jesus, for over twenty-four hours I've been asking You to save my mare. She's probably not going to live through the night and I don't understand why You won't answer my prayer. You know how much I love her. Can't You just take the foal and leave her for me?"

Somewhere inside I had the vague idea that if I offered the foal as a sacrifice, God might spare Morning Mist's life. In counseling that is known as "bargaining," but I wasn't thinking as a professional at the moment.

As I once again waited for the vet I continued my dialogue with God, saying I didn't know what He was doing, couldn't see His overall plan for this personal tragedy, but I was willing to trust Him to bring good out of it. God must have heard that weak prayer. As I knelt there, my face in my hands, I was aware of a strange peace that came over me. In the midst of this tragedy I felt a peace I'd never known before.

From somewhere I found the strength to utter words that surprised me. "Lord, I *know* that what You want is the best for my life. If what You really want is Morning Mist, You don't have to take her—I *give* her to You. You are second to nothing. Even though this doesn't make sense to me, I give You this friend that I love so dearly."

From the driveway, I could hear a car door closing. Dr. Hall met me at the back door. "I'm sorry, Doctor," I said, beginning to cry again, "but I just can't come with you. It's too horrible for me to see her again."

He disappeared into the darkness without me, and was back in minutes. "She's in terrible pain. Crazy with fever, too. No way will she make it till morning. I'm sorry, but I have to put her down."

I couldn't utter a word. I just nodded, understanding that she had to be put out of her pain.

With an aching heart I sat at the kitchen table and waited for ten long minutes. And then Dr. Hall shuffled through the back door. Glumly, he said, "I was able to inject her in the neck. It only took a few minutes. She's gone. I'm awfully sorry for you, Susan. I can see how much you loved her."

He said he would send a truck in the morning for her remains. I nodded, thanked him, and watched his headlights back out the drive. Then I dropped my head and sobbed and sobbed.

I had lost my friend and companion, the last treasured thing I had on earth.

After a time, I phoned Jeanie in Chicago, though it was almost four o'clock in the morning. Graciously, she stayed on the phone with me for a long time as we tried to make sense of why this had happened. Why had God allowed this to happen? After talking and crying for over an hour we hung up without any definitive answers.

As I fell into bed a strange, stray thought came to me—certainly not from my own poor, befogged head: When I aborted my baby, I had been giving up the life of the child to save myself, and it didn't work. I'd only found pain and spiritual death. In the same way I had offered God the life of the foal in exchange for the life of my mare. Was that a camouflage? Had I been trying to protect something dear, something He really wanted me to sacrifice to Him?

I was too weary to wrestle with all that and soon fell asleep.

But in the coming days the truth became clear.

"Coincidentally," I had agreed to meet Dan at his parents' home for a special family celebration the weekend following Morning Mist's death. Dan had been after me for several weeks to come, and though I was reluctant, I went.

Throughout the weekend I felt uncomfortable in Dan's presence. In the past I had been almost addicted to this relationship, but now all my feelings for Dan seemed to be melting away. He was still a kind, sensitive person—but my desire to be with him was fading with every minute. The understanding that this was an "addiction" I had to surrender to God was extraordinarily strong.

All I could think of was a Bible verse I had read in First Corinthians about being made "a new creation," about allowing "old things" to pass away.

That was when my mind cleared about the week's events. God *had* been trying to reach me with a crucial message. Stubbornly, I had hung onto the relationship with Dan when it was clearly wrong. Oh, I'd made it look good. I had avoided sexual contact. I had paraded all of Dan's good qualities before God. But the relationship was wrong from the start. It had borne bad fruit—an affair, an abortion, a marriage destroyed. In God's eyes it never would be right.

I realized the heavy cost that had just been paid—the life of my prized horse—to reach my unwilling heart with that message. I was awed and humbled. And I knew what I had to do.

I broke the news to Dan on Sunday afternoon while walking in the woods near his parents' home. The words came more easily than I'd imagined possible. He could not understand why we had to end our relationship, and he looked miserable. Even the unhappiness on his face and his imploring did not change my mind.

Our parting was tense and uncomfortable. I knew I would never see him again—and even with the sense of God's presence with me, it was hard.

On the plane back to Detroit I felt sadness, but mostly relief. There was joy in knowing that God was truly about the business of making me a "new creation." Sweeping out the old to make room for the new.

Briefly, as I stepped from the plane, I had the fleeting impression that this was just preparation for what now lay ahead. I felt—what was it?—a "calling"? Retrieving my luggage, I couldn't say exactly. I just knew it was something very, very important.

9
THE CALL

Almost six years were to pass before I felt that inner stirring again. I pursued my career in the academic world, rising to Assistant Vice-President at Wayne State University. Little did I suspect that another jolt—one of life's awful surprises—would catapult me into my special "calling." All in all, the fact that it was a surprise was probably best, because I never would have chosen the path on my own.

The years between my healing in 1976 and this sudden turn of events in 1982 were ordinary enough. However, every bit of it was preparation for what was to come. They were years of progressive deepening in my understanding of the Lord's ways.

In Detroit I had developed a few close friendships, but one special friend I'd found was instrumental in helping me to grow as a Christian. Brad was a graduate student, a good-looking Texan, slow of speech but quick to help me see God's perspective whenever I had a conflict with another faculty member or student. Each week we met for prayer and, with his encouragement, I slowly learned what God has to say in His Word, the Bible, and how to put His directives into practice.

All of which was vital considering what happened next. Still climbing the academic ladder, I attended the Harvard Business School's program for senior university managers during the summer of 1981. Then I accepted a position as Dean of the College at a small liberal arts school in Maine, which was tucked in the middle of the rolling hills and blue lakes of that wild and gorgeous state. Maine felt like home to me, and I would escape to the seashore whenever possible to walk the sand dunes, to rest, and to listen for the voice of God in the crashing breakers and the cry of the gulls.

Not that I got to the shore often. Like many small colleges, this one had hit a financial slump. My first year as Dean of the College was a very rigorous and demanding one. The financial crisis we faced was so bad that in May the Board of Directors and college staff voted a fifty percent pay cut for everyone for the duration of the 1982 summer.

It was after this tough but rewarding year on a new academic "team" that I decided to attend a "Partners' Retreat" at Oral Roberts University. I had supported the Roberts healing ministry for several years and had already attended one retreat on the beautiful campus in Tulsa in 1980. That had been a gentle time of rest and spiritual growth. I was hoping for a similar tranquil time as I stepped off the plane in Tulsa on a sweltering afternoon in June 1982.

The bus to take us to O.R.U. had not even arrived yet

when I felt a strange urgency to step away from the crowd of partners gathered outside the airport. The sun was scorching, and I moved away from the group to lean against the shaded stone wall of the terminal building. From inside me, a simple prayer rose: *Lord, I've come here to get away from the pressures at the college. I need the rest. But more than that, I need to sense Your presence within me.*

And then, unbidden and surprising, the thought formed: *After five years of learning about You, Lord, I'm ready. Yes, Lord, I'm ready and want a closer walk with You. Lead me, Jesus, and show me the way.*

The bus arrived shortly. Curiously, the weekend at O.R.U. was uneventful, except for the deep sense of peace that hovered about me, the conviction that God was very close to me at that time. The only thing that stood out was a vague feeling I had while touring Roberts' then-new City of Faith hospital complex. It was as if the word *healing* was echoing in the depths of my being.

Still, when I returned to Maine, it was to continue my academic pursuits—certainly not a "healing" ministry. The fall '82 semester would be business as usual. Or so I imagined.

Throughout the summer things at the college turned sour. Then, three weeks into the semester, I was called into the President's office and stunned by his announcement.

"Susan," he began, "I've decided that we're not working well as a team. Furthermore, one of us has to go, and guess who it is."

I smiled. The President often dismayed the staff with his strange sense of humor. Was this some kind of joke? I attempted a chuckle in my voice as my palms grew clammy.

"Last year was great—and our whole staff all pulled together through a tough summer. So will you please explain what you're saying?"

"I mean you're finished. Your job here is over."

I couldn't believe it. "But you gave me a great review in May. We've worked through so many problems together. If I've made some mistakes you haven't told me about before, don't I get a 'warning period' to address whatever is bothering you?"

"There's no discussion about this," he said in a clipped, dismissing tone.

"But it's so *unfair*." Something like a cold nuclear explosion was going on in my stomach. "How will I find a job this time of year—?"

"*I have my reasons*," he interrupted, an angry edge cutting through his cool demeanor. "So that's *it* for today. We'll talk later." And then he summarily motioned me toward the door.

I could not face the rest of the day on campus. Giving some lame excuse to my secretary, I walked to my car and slumped behind the steering wheel. *Jesus?* I prayed. *Where are You? How can You be allowing this unfair man to rule against me—like some dictator? And for no reason. What's going to happen to me? It's going to look so bad, being tossed out on my ear, when I try to land another job.*

I felt helpless. That evening, I went to visit Kevin, a professor from the college, and his wife, Beth. They were strong Christians, and had been supportive in the year since

I had arrived. I knew they'd be sitting down to supper when I showed up, but I couldn't bear being alone.

They were shocked and angry at the news. Kevin predicted that the faculty would be in an uproar when they heard what had happened. Several times that evening I broke into tears. When Kevin and Beth had calmed down from their initial reaction, they were able to pray with me, and promised their continued support. God, we decided, must have some plan afoot, though I couldn't fathom leaving the academic world.

What would I do besides academics? I wondered. All through October, while I walked the rugged Maine coastline, or meandered through the fall forests, trying to hear God's direction for my life, I wondered. That time of quietness, like the retreat at O.R.U., was to be a time of preparation—of sweeping away my own professional goals and plans so they could be replaced with something bigger.

During that fall I also attended a weekly Bible study in Kevin and Beth's church. How I needed the support of other Christian men and women, people I could pray for and who prayed for me regularly and cared for me when I felt so unsure about my future.

It was during our time of prayer one evening that a funny little thought kept cropping up. *Be ready to move.* And one name kept coming, that of the fast-developing coastal city, *Portland.* Less than two hours north of Boston, this old harbor town was attracting lots of professionals and developers, and the idea—wherever it was coming from—intrigued me.

The prayer group agreed to pray for me while I took a three-day trip to Portland, "just to check out the possibility of setting up a counseling practice there."

Maybe I was hoping I would walk into some counselor's office to a red-carpet invitation to join a successful established practice. That was not to be. But as I priced office space and housing, the solid assurance formed within me that I was definitely to move to Portland.

And do what? I prayed during the drive home.

To work in healing, came the reply.

The thought jolted me. *Healing? But how do I support myself?*

Again, the enigmatic words, *Trust Me.*

With both excitement and fear, I made the move to Portland, signing a lease on a small downtown office that seemed just right. The Lord repeatedly seemed to be saying, "This will be a small beginning, but just lean on Me." It felt so uneasy to be uprooting again so soon after my big move from the Midwest. I imagined what Peter must have felt like when he was asked to leave his fishing nets and follow Jesus. The academic life I had known for years, the world where I was comfortable, was now behind me. Yet the inner assurance always came. *These are the small beginnings of the work planned for you. Like the tiny mustard seed, it will grow in time.*

In time. It was a cold, lean winter. I lived mainly off my savings, and spent days knocking on the doors of priests, ministers, family and divorce attorneys, and other counselors—anyone who might give me some client referrals. By February, my office phone was ringing—from time to time, anyway.

And still I waited for the proverbial "other shoe" to drop. One month later, I caught my first glimpse of the road ahead of me.

In March I was asked to speak at the monthly meeting of the Order of St. Luke the Physician, a group interested in Christ's healing today. I had met the chaplain of the organization and mentioned—excluding the details—the fact that I had experienced a tremendous spiritual and emotional healing myself.

When I stood up before this group of interdenominational believers in the healing ministry, I was not expecting the strong nudge that came. *Tell them your whole story.*

That couldn't be God—could it? *Oh, no,* I retorted, gripping the podium. *Not all of it.*

Yes. All of it.

Not about the abortion. The very thought made my knees weak. The chaplain was eyeing me curiously, wondering at my hesitation.

Yes. About the abortion also.

Obedience was the only reason I dared broach my humbling past.

For the next half-hour or so, I told my story—all of it—to this room of collegial professionals and lay people. A peace had taken control so that I was not even shaking when I got to the part about the abortion and planned suicide. Around the room eyes glistened with tears. There was no fidgeting or restlessness from word one until the end, when I concluded: "The healing love of Jesus Christ reached down and picked me up out of the pit and literally saved my life. All of my professional training as a psychologist could not help rescue me from the abyss of self-hatred and guilt. God used a supportive Christian to touch me and heal the pain. Instantaneously, when I finally turned to Him, He took away my terrible inner torment. And I believe the same healing is available to all of us."

With that I concluded. There was a moment of silence—then applause. Loud and prolonged clapping accompanied me back to my seat, followed by the chaplain's grateful thanks. When the meeting broke up, there were warm remarks, and handshakes from many in the audience.

And then she approached me, a woman whose face I had noticed during my talk because of its absolute blankness. Fleetingly, I had feared she was judging me because of my "confession." Now there she stood in her fashionable suit, her hand outstretched, with pain tracing its furrow on her forehead.

"Thank you," she said quietly, gripping my hand. "I could not have done what you did. You see"—and she glanced over her shoulder to be sure we were out of anyone's earshot—"several years ago I had an abortion." Her lips quivered ever so slightly. "I haven't been able to forgive myself. Maybe we can talk sometime. Maybe you can help me." Then she pivoted and was gone, leaving me stunned. She was the picture of success, she looked entirely "together." How could she be—

My thoughts were interrupted by a second woman, slightly older, who had slipped away from a group by the door the moment she saw the first woman leave me.

She was the second of *three* women who approached me

in the aftermath of my talk. When the last one walked up, I recognized the look of pain and was a little more ready to hear her confess to having had an abortion also.

As I contemplated this outpouring of anguished souls that evening, the questions came: *How many more women out there are suffering from the wrong choice they made at fifteen, or twenty-six, or thirty-four, to terminate a pregnancy by abortion? How many have killed off part of their psyches in order to survive the horrible, if late, realization that instead of giving life, they have given death?*

On the Wednesday following my first talk I received an invitation from a professional group in the area. The man who phoned said he had heard about my "experience," and the talk I'd given to the Order of St. Luke. Could I address their organization as well?

I heard myself agree. Then I hung up the phone and wanted to kick myself around the office several times. *You are not going to run around showing all the skeletons in your closet to the whole community,* I argued. *This time show a little more restraint.*

Nonetheless, as I walked to the podium, the inner directive was clear: *The whole story, Susan.* I fought it, wondering if I had masochistic tendencies.

Still, the same peace seized me. And the story flowed out naturally.

Again I was amazed at the response. This time there were two women who lingered at the edge of the room long enough to catch me alone. As one of them stated it, "I have so much unfinished business regarding my abortion. I hope you continue what you're doing. For some of us, there's not much left inside. Someone's got to start building us up again."

Continue what I'm doing. Someone to build us up again. Those words haunted me—at home, in the office, during church—for weeks. I didn't like what I thought I was hearing. I wasn't about to hang out a shingle for that kind of healing.

But I couldn't escape the image: On one side was God, His hands extended in forgiveness; and on the other side were thousands of broken-hearted women, aching to hear the words that would resurrect them from spiritual and emotional death: *Go and sin no more. Your sins are forgiven you.*

There was another mental image—the kind face of my heavenly Father, asking: *Do you love Me totally, unconditionally? Do you love Me enough to care for the ones I'm sending to you?*

I didn't have to hang out a shingle. Very soon, the broken and wounded were coming to my doorstep.

One of the first was Jacqueline. As my practice grew in my first year in Portland I was rarely surprised by the handsome, stylish, successful-looking people who came to disclose their glaring anguish. Pain knows no cultural or economic barriers. But Jacqueline *was* a surprise.

Jacqueline was a young woman struggling, on the surface at least, to mend her crumbling marriage. She was articulate and educated. Her "presenting problem," the thing she had come to get help with, supposedly, was the fact that her husband was inattentive, cold. Most of the time she feared his violent temper, especially since he had struck her on two or three occasions. On the surface it seemed to be the ideal marriage of two professionals, but it was rotten underneath.

The Call

The fact that she feared his anger was caused by something she had done, might have tipped me off. From her quavering voice and the way she twisted her handkerchief anxiously as she spoke, I knew the tension was building to get all the facts "out on the table."

On Jacqueline's fourth visit she dropped her "bomb." It is a professionally recognized pattern that for some clients the true reason for their seeking help may surface after several sessions and just minutes before they are ready to walk out the door. Pretty, well-attired, "together" Jacqueline had already picked up her leather handbag and gotten out the keys to her Mercedes, when she paused at the edge of her seat.

"There's something I've been meaning to tell you," she began, her eyes avoiding mine. "I'm sure you'll hate me. But some years ago I had an abortion."

The last word was a lance, piercing the boil-like agony she had concealed. Instead of getting up to leave, Jacqueline began sobbing uncontrollably.

Minutes passed and I sat quietly as she wept into her monogrammed handkerchief. Behind the loveliness, so much pain. When at last she grew silent, I asked, "Why do you think I'll hate you?"

Now, almost dispassionately, she managed to say, "Because I hate myself so much. I'll never be able to forgive myself."

I had no doubt that's how she felt. We were well past the end of her session and I felt the pressure of my next scheduled client, yet I did not want Jacqueline to leave without some hint of hope.

Now I was aware of picking my way over cautious ground. Not that I was embarrassed about my faith, but I wasn't about to force my beliefs on my patients. Jacqueline's sophistication, schooling, and strong personality had not given her the tools to work through her guilt. Nor would they ever.

While Jacqueline clutched her handbag and continued to stare, I said, "The only hope I have found in fully forgiving ourselves is in allowing God to reach down and touch us. I'd like very much to help you deal with your pain. If you're interested I'd like to share with you at our next session some principles regarding forgiveness I feel really work."

Her face brightened just a little. "Certainly. Next session then."

When she had gone, it was my turn to think about heading for the door. *Lord, what am I going to say to Jacqueline when she comes back? I've experienced Your touch, but how can I help her experience it, too? I'm not an evangelist, just a counselor.*

And I was not concerned for Jacqueline alone. Within a short time, other women came to me with the same "hidden" problem among their other "presenting" issues.

One was Janie, a nineteen-year-old who had become sexually active several years before as a sophomore in high school. Slumped in the overstuffed chair in my office, she revealed that her boyfriend had pressured her to go to bed with him. Janie knew little about birth control and two months later she missed her period. After missing her second and third, she went to some girlfriends in a panic. She was surprised to learn that two of them had had abortions.

"Don't sweat it," they had told her. "If you're pregnant, we'll get you fixed."

Getting "fixed" was the most excruciating experience in Janie's young life. Not only was there the physical pain of the abortionist's "tools" for a second trimester abortion but now she felt she had no future, nothing to live for. She had some justifiable fear that she might not be able to get pregnant again—but that was a more remote problem just now, because she distrusted men and avoided the attentions of several who were interested in her. Janie's "presenting" problem was depression. It had taken her only two visits to spill the real, abiding problem.

And there was Sabrina, forty-two years old and terrified, she told me, of reentering the job market now that her children were all in school. She had fulfilled her family's expectations of her and now she felt unneeded, useless. Initially, I worked on her need to trust in her abilities and encouraged her to take on small tasks outside the home to begin rebuilding her self-confidence. But there was a blockage somewhere. Her deep disclosure, when it finally came out, pulled at my heartstrings despite my professional years of hearing personal "confessions."

Several sessions into our discussion of her feelings of failure, she stopped mid-sentence. "The truth is, I've got to find something to do that's worth getting up for every day. You see, I feel pretty worthless."

And through tears, the story of her abortion came out. At thirty-seven she had found herself pregnant. It was unplanned and she dreaded the idea of starting all over with an infant when her two children were already in high school. Her husband shrugged when she asked his opinion. He wasn't interested in another child and besides, he said, it was her body and she had the right to choose what happened to it.

Sabrina swallowed his reply "hook, line, and sinker," especially since it sounded so much like what she was reading by the media about the pro-abortionist's rhetoric. Still, she struggled with her decision for five months until she made the last-minute decision to abort. She was in no way prepared for the living nightmare.

After the doctor injected her with saline solution, she was left alone on a stretcher for an hour-and-a-half, feeling the child in her womb fighting and kicking as it was slowly burned to death. Though she sobbed for days afterward, she felt there was no way to free herself from the penetrating guilt of having murdered her baby.

"It is too late for me," she concluded despondently. Her voice sounded like a lost soul crying from a barren wilderness. Time, she said, had failed to heal her wounded spirit, even though the counselor at the abortion clinic had told her the feelings would eventually fade.

One of the things I was unprepared for, as more and more hurting women came to me throughout the spring and summer of 1983, was my own reaction to hearing about their abortions. For years, I had felt that God had healed me. I no longer felt guilt, I was totally set free. But just what technique was I to use with my clients to bring them God's healing from their own abortions? Talking *at* them and telling them my own personal experience did not feel adequate. I prayed fervently for some wisdom.

As I searched for just what would be the most appropriate professional tools to use with these clients I decided to review any research literature that had been done with post-abortion women. Some of what I learned surprised me, but much of what I found merely confirmed what I was seeing in my own practice. The following is a brief representation of what I found.

Depending on the situation the research shows that most women suffer one or several of the following symptoms after an abortion: unresolved grief, chronic guilt, anniversary depression, psychosomatic illness, drug and alcohol abuse, suicide attempts, psychotic breakdowns, or other lesser resultant effects.

One of the most universal aftereffects of abortion is the feeling of guilt and loss. In my own practice some post-abortion women may initially deny feeling guilty and consequently avoid the topic of their abortions early on in the counseling relationship. However, invariably the topic comes up, perhaps around the anniversary due date or death date. When I've asked my clients how they feel about it in retrospect more than 90 percent share they feel some level of guilty feelings. Other women, who perhaps have come to counseling with the presenting problem being the aftereffects of their abortion, define their feelings ranging from a pervasive dullness or depression to overpowering remorse and regret.

In an article titled "The Rising Cost of Abortion" (*Medi-*

cal Hypoanalysis, Spring 1980), Sexton and Maddox found in a study of 64 women they treated who had had abortions, in every case the abortion was determined to be their major life offending event. Aftereffects included psychosis, severe depression, and self-destructive behavior.

The latter is an all-too-frequent thought that a high percentage of post-abortion women have contemplated. In a study of 4000 women, done by Suiciders Anonymous, 45 percent who had attempted suicide had had an abortion. In my practice I have seen many, many women who've reported suicidal impulses when reliving in their mind the scenes of their abortions.

Of the women that I've seen who had abortions during their teenage years, the strong majority say they did so in a panic response when they found out they were pregnant. Too often little time was put into thinking through their various options. Many today who regret their decision have said they wish abortion had not been so readily available, or presented by friends and family as the "quick fix" alternative. Little if anything was ever presented to them about the long-lasting psychological and physiological scars that would result from abortion.

In a study in the *New England Journal of Medicine* (Sept. 1983) titled "Risks Associated with Teenage Abortion," Cates, Schultz, and Grimes report that risks of cervical trauma are greater for young teenagers and nulliparous women, those who have not previously borne children. They go on to say that . . . "their findings cause concern because cervical injury in initial unplanned pregnancies may predispose young women to adverse outcomes in future planned pregnancies."

It's been my observation that many teenagers today, feeling little responsibility, see the ready availability of abortion as the automatic choice, instead of taking the time to study all of the information available about abortion and its aftereffects. Unfortunately, this statement can be made too frequently about women of all ages who choose to have an abortion.

As I looked through the research literature on the psychological aftereffects of abortion, I was also struck by some of the more dramatic physical post-abortion patterns that were being discovered. A study later conducted by the Department of Public Health at Boston's Preterm Clinic in 1984 revealed that 43 percent of the women obtaining abortions had already had a previous abortion. Women were choosing to use abortion as a form of birth control despite the fact that research shows multiple abortions increase the risk of complications in future pregnancies.

In fact, as early as June 1980, Levin, Schoenbaum, et al., reported in the *Journal of the American Medical Association* that 35 percent of women who had had two or more abortions lost their next pregnancy by miscarriage. Other research shows that post-abortion infections occur in 2.5 to 17 percent of women who've had abortions. Even a minor infection can cause serious damage and some infections can lead to sterility, infertility, or ectopic pregnancy, which is a tubal pregnancy. Specifically, Brenner, Roy, and Mishell in a *JAMA* article in 1980 titled "Ectopic Pregnancy" found that women who've had two or more abortions have a four times greater risk of having an ectopic pregnancy. Similarly, Creasy and Herron report in "Prevention of Preterm Birth" (*Seminars in Perinatology*, July 1981) that every abortion increases the risk of premature birth later and in the case of a second trimester abortion the risk is increased fivefold.

10
INNER HEALING

Having read all that I could find in post-abortion research that week after counseling with Jacqueline, I became more convinced than ever that I needed to find the right counseling techniques to appropriately help women through their unresolved grief, loss, and depression. Then I heard about a conference in Rutland, Vermont, on something called Inner Healing or Healing of Memories. The conference speakers were Francis and Judith MacNutt, internationally known for their work in this exciting area.

Inner healing, I learned at the conference, is a cross-disciplinary counseling tool that combines techniques from the field of psychology with principles of Jesus' healing power. Agnes Sanford, the woman who pioneered the concept of Inner Healing in the 1950s, felt that traditional psychotherapy tried to help individuals "process" or work through past psychological traumas—but often missed the mark.

Too often the emotional scar is never healed. The individual simply learns how to live with it a little more easily.

As Judith MacNutt, a trained psychologist, and Francis, a former Catholic priest, taught us the theory of inner healing, I wondered how I could possibly use this with my clients. Hearing them talk about it, I realized that I had had an inner healing experience alone on my knees in 1976 though I hadn't known what to call it. It was not until the end of the conference, when Judith led an inner healing service, that I saw the effectiveness of this tool.

The service entailed Judith's leading the audience in prayer using the psychological tool of guided mental imagery to lead them back in their memories to the scene of some psychological trauma. For example, one man in his forties was able to replay in his mind the night when his father, having come home drunk, beat him severely with a leather belt and told him he was dirt. Since that time, he had clutched whenever he faced an opportunity to advance in school or in work. After all, if his own father thought he was dirt, how could he possibly succeed?

Once Judith helped him to reconstruct that past painful scene, she said, surprisingly, "Now picture Jesus walking into that room with you and your father." From that instant, I could sense a mighty Presence right there at the conference. As Jesus entered the picture, the man was able to deeply and fully forgive his father and tears of cleansing flowed.

The conference turned out to be one of the most moving experiences of my professional life. But still I wondered, as I drove back to Portland, about this process of inner healing.

Could it *begin* to touch the pain and guilt of the post-abortion women who were coming to me for solace? About eight in ten of my patients expressed a belief in God. Perhaps, with courage, I could introduce them to this healing God. And then I remembered my week's calendar: One of my first patients on Monday was Jacqueline. I did not want to misstep with her.

When Jacqueline came, fashionably attired as always, my remarks about her impeccable appearance went ignored. Everything about her asked the awesome question: What can you do to help me?

Lord, I prayed, closing the door to the outer office, *if You've led me into this, don't desert me now.*

At my initial intake interview I had gained some knowledge about Jacqueline's faith background. Her family had belonged to a denominational church, but when she reached high school, going to church or staying in bed on Sunday morning was her choice. She had abandoned church then, for all practical purposes, except when she wanted stained glass and a booming organ for her wedding ceremony.

I started our session this day with an open-ended question about faith once again. In a critical, self-judging tone Jacqueline responded, "I feel I've failed God pretty miserably."

"We *all* have," I jumped in, trying to lift her up. "Don't you see? That's why He sent His Son, Jesus, to die in our place. He lived the perfect life where none of us could. Now, because of His sacrifice, you and I can come back to

God, no matter what we've done against Him, or against ourselves or anybody."

It was too much, too soon, perhaps. The blank look on Jacqueline's face told me that theology was beyond her, or else she couldn't imagine God even *wanting* her to come to Him.

"Jacqueline," I pursued, "I don't want to force anything on you. But I would like to use a tool in our counseling that combines psychology and faith."

She looked uncertain. Then, dutifully, she nodded slightly and said with a shrug, "Well . . . if you think it will help."

"I do believe it will help, and as long as you have a faith that God exists, then leave the rest to me. Just sit back, close your eyes, and relax. We are going to use both your memory and your imagination as we journey back in time."

Presently she nodded.

Taking a deep breath, I asked her to picture the room in the clinic where her abortion took place. Minutes of silence followed. Her face was stony-white.

"Can you see what you are wearing?" Another nod.

"Can you see the expression on your face?"

Jacqueline's lips tightened. Something like disgust, hatred, pain marred her beautiful face. It was a revelation of her innermost soul.

"Now, I want you to imagine that Jesus has just walked into the room. Can you see Him, Jacqueline? He's looking at you with the most loving eyes you've ever seen."

At once, an anguished and longing expression molded

her features—as though she wanted to hide and be embraced at the same time.

"You know by looking into His eyes what He wants to say. In your memory, walk over to Him and let Him embrace you." Her lip was quivering, and I hoped this was not turning out to be too much for her to take. Still I felt compelled to continue. "Now I want you to look at Him again and listen to what He has to say to you."

Her lips twisted and a heart-wrenching sob escaped. A lump filled my throat. Jacqueline's perfectly applied makeup was smearing as the tears flowed.

"He is saying . . . 'I . . . forgive you,' " she managed.

For long minutes, her face buried in her hands, Jacqueline sobbed and sobbed. I reached out my hand and touched her arm and prayed in silence while Jesus did His healing work. At some point I could sense that the tears of pain became cleansing tears. After some time, she pulled out her monogrammed handkerchief to blot the streams that continued to flow silently down her cheeks. I let the silence wrap us like a blanket, not wanting to disrupt the sanctity of these precious healing moments when God was reaching right into her womb and her spirit to give her new life.

When Jacqueline could speak again, she was able to tell me in her articulate way about the amazing thing that had happened inside her.

"The moment when I looked into His eyes was awful. Not because there was hatred—but because of the incredible, beautiful love I saw in Him. He was looking right inside of me. I wanted to say I was so, so sorry—to ask His forgiveness. But there was no need for words. Before I'd even made a confession, He said, 'I forgive you.' And," she said, choking up again, "that's when I broke."

We talked for a while longer and then closed our session for that day. I told her to spend some quiet time each day of the upcoming week remembering the healing beauty of her journey with Jesus. I explained that while the event of her abortion would never change, Jesus had just melted away all the pain in its memory.

The coming weeks and months saw me walking through similar experiences with other women who had known the horror of abortion. Janie and Sabrina both began the process of healing when they met Jesus in encounters not unlike Jacqueline's. Whether a woman had been religious or not, I was amazed that each one who fully opened herself to the inner journey heard a variation of the words, "I forgive you." For some of them there was still much work to do in mending fractured marriages, broken self-images, or relationships with children. But from the light of hope I saw in their eyes, I knew they were beginning anew on solid footing. That knowledge filled me with unspeakable joy.

I wish I could say that every single woman who came seeking help in the painful aftermath of her abortion experience was so wonderfully set free of pain. That was not so. I am compelled to say, however, that the women who were willing to seek help from God and not merely from a bag of psychological tricks found healing in much higher percentages than those who held a hard, clinical perspective.

Thus I learned that my being fired from the college was

not happenstance or "bad luck," but a sharp, hurtful turn that threw me at first. Now I understand that it took getting thrown to open my eyes to the need that lay all around me. As I walked the streets of Portland, passing society matrons or teenage girls in blue jeans, I realized that any one of them might walk into my office at any time. *Any one* of these women, from any walk of life, might be suffering from the emotional and spiritual death a woman undergoes when she submits to abortion. So many needed healing.

The Jacqueline who walked into my office the week after our inner healing session was hardly recognizable. The nicely styled hair and manicured nails were the same, but it was the light that radiated from her face that made my heart leap for joy.

She began talking before she'd even lighted on the office sofa. "It's absolutely incredible, Susan. I can't believe what's happened."

I sat back in my chair and just listened.

"As you directed my thoughts, I could see the whole scene again. I felt that sickening fear," she said, cradling her stomach. "Even worse, there was this searing hatred for myself and what I was doing. But it was too late. The abortion was over and the doctor had turned his back and left. I was alone—so alone. You don't know how much I felt doomed."

I smiled, thinking, *Oh, yes, I do know.*

"And then you said His name—Jesus. In my mind I looked up and saw Him walk through the door. And His eyes. They were like oceans. They held all my pain. I felt I could drown in the love. I'd never known Jesus like that in the years I went to church. I felt He was rather . . . aloof, uninterested in me personally.

"But you said I would hear what He was telling me. And"—again the tears were coming, happy tears—"I'll never forget it in a million years. He said, 'I forgive you.' Since then, I've been free of the hatred. Oh, Susan, I've never been religious at all, but now I find I want to know more about God. I never realized He loved me this much."

By this time I was beaming. We talked for a while longer, addressing the problems of abuse she was experiencing in her marriage. There was still much to do in that area, but at least I would be working with a whole person now, not the fragmented, guilt-ridden Jacqueline who first came to me. She was going to make it, and we could address the problems in her marriage with God's help.

I felt good about what I was seeing unfold. I had found the first keys to help heal post-abortion women of their guilt and loss. I suspected, personally, that there was more for me to yet learn. A small something still felt not quite finished from my own abortion and still had a hold on me.

But that hold was about to be broken once and for all.

11
FOREVER HIS

After the wonderful session with Jacqueline, I did not feel so upbeat about a woman who was referred to me the following week. A former client called and asked if I would visit a middle-aged friend of hers named Betty who had been hospitalized in the psychiatric ward of Maine Medical Center. Since the woman was under the care of a psychiatrist who was able to dispense medications, I hesitated at first. But then I felt that now-familiar inner nudge to go. What harm could just one visit do?

When I walked into Betty's room in the psych ward, my attention was riveted on her eyes. Though her conversation was lucid and coherent, I felt pain every time I saw the dull lifelessness in her otherwise pretty eyes. She talked in a listless monotone, the voice that belongs to those without hope. It was the second time she had been admitted that year. I learned that her husband had deserted her for another woman and her children were now grown and gone.

The emotional tension had worn her down until she felt she was cracking.

After a brief conversation I learned she was able to sign herself out of the hospital on day passes, and I suggested she might come and see me in an office visit. She agreed to come the following week.

Betty walked into my office with the same flat look in her eyes I had seen in the hospital. Her shoulders sagged as if she were staggering under the weight of a double-heavy burden. And no wonder. Her story, as it unfolded, was truly tragic.

For years her husband had beaten her, though no one else knew about the abuse. "Before that he 'beat' me emotionally, so what did the physical beating matter?" she observed without emotion. She had withdrawn from him and he began to tell her she was crazy. Three years of therapy followed, but the situation only grew worse. She said she'd never really been able to fully trust her therapist, even though he had been kind.

The therapy uncovered earlier scars from abuse Betty had suffered as a girl. As she continued, a gruesome picture of her family life emerged. Her father had often beaten her under the guise of discipline. She had come to hate her father and could not forgive him for the torture he had inflicted upon her.

I recognized a pattern that is familiar to counselors: For complicated reasons, a child who is abused can be drawn to marry a person who turns out to be an abusive spouse. Probing for possible connections, I brought her back to her present nuclear family and asked about her children and where they were now.

"I have two children," Betty began. She paused and added, "But I could have had more."

"What do you mean?"

"Before my husband and I were married we were involved physically and I got pregnant. He didn't want to marry me right away. I knew that if my father found out I was pregnant he would kill me—maybe literally. I thought it was the only thing to do at the time, so I had an abortion." I witnessed the faintest flicker of emotion. "I've been slowly dying inside ever since."

Now I could see beyond the flat grayness in her eyes. I was humbled by the childlike vulnerability, the "little girl" hurt that showed—especially when she volunteered that she had never felt safe enough to share the secret about her abortion with anyone else.

Several visits followed, and each time I could sense the crushing weight Betty bore. Her depression was far more severe than Jacqueline's. I wondered what it would take to unlock the pain, heal the scars.

Just around the time Betty and I began meeting, in the spring of 1984, I received a phone call from my dear friend Maria in Chicago. Of course I had no way of knowing at the time, but that phone call was going to help unlock the mystery of Betty—and provide the answer to a personal feeling that had nagged me for several months.

I was pleased to hear Maria's voice, and even more thrilled when she told me that she and Jack were coordinating a Healing Conference featuring the MacNutts and a priest from Loyola University, Father Bob Sears. It took little arm-twisting to get me to agree to register for the conference.

The opening meetings of the conference surpassed my highest expectations. Again, I was amazed at the professionalism the MacNutts brought to their work. But the remark that intrigued me most came during Father Sears' lecture on "Healing the Family Tree," a concept first pioneered by Dr. Ken McAll, a British psychiatrist.

He talked about the importance of introducing the Lord's healing power into unresolved issues in the family experience. Then, almost as an aside, he mentioned how important it was to hold a committal service for miscarried or aborted babies. Spiritually, he explained, these souls needed to be given over to rest eternally with God so that, for the living, tremendous healing could follow in their families.

What a revolutionary, magnificent idea, I thought. Now my own inner nudge felt like a sharp elbow in the ribs. But I had experienced healing. Could there be something more for me?

Following the talk I approached Father Sears, and he agreed to meet me that evening and tell me more about his theory.

At seven P.M., we met in the chapel of the conference center. I was relaxed immediately by Father Sears' warm and unjudgmental nature, drawn by his open smile. Perhaps it was his kindness that made me turn the conversation from theory to actuality. At once I found myself unfolding all the details of my own pregnancy and abortion, including the subsequent healing.

Quietly he nodded and listened unhurriedly. Once I'd finished he suggested we have a committal service. I needed little prompting. "Will you close your eyes, sit back, and relax now, Susan?"

I agreed and leaned back in the pew. At first it felt a little odd being the "client" for a change. But, with my eyes shut, I focused on his gentle voice.

"Picture yourself as you looked during that summer you had the abortion. You are seated somewhere in your home."

In my mind's eye, I was back in our country home, sitting in the chair by the fireplace. It was like being in a museum room that had been shut away from the passage of time. My hair was styled as it had been at that time and, interestingly, I was wearing a print blouse I had long since discarded.

"Feel the feelings of that time."

A cold blade of loneliness pierced me. Separatedness. Instinctively I knew the scene was post-abortion.

"Now, Susan, look up in that memory and find Jesus standing there."

He was standing in the middle of the carpet. Vaguely I had the impression of sandaled feet, a white robe. But then there were His eyes! His face was radiant, full of love, smiling.

"Do you see what He's holding in His arms? It's a baby wrapped in a blanket."

My heart began to beat faster.

"Do you have any sense of the sex of the child?"

I hadn't noted it at first, but the blanket was pale blue. My heart leaped. At the core of my being I had always sensed that my baby was a boy.

"A boy," I managed. A lump was tightening my throat.

"Then picture Jesus holding that little boy."

His peach-fuzz head brushed against Jesus' chest. Tiny hands were moving in random, infant motions. I could almost hear the gurgling and cooing.

Tears were streaming by this time, running off my chin, even dampening my skirt as they landed in my lap. The loneliness I had felt was not just because I had separated myself from my beliefs and from those who loved me—it was separation from my own little one.

"Do you have a sense of the child's name?"

Strange question. I was about to shake my head when an answer escaped unbidden from my lips. "His name is Jeremy."

"What a lovely name," replied Father Sears. "Now, Susan, I want you to go and stand in front of Jesus and Jeremy. Why don't you tell them what's on your heart?"

The tears were now a flood. Spontaneously the words came. "Oh, Jeremy, I love you very much. I'm so sorry for what I did. I hope you can forgive me and love me, too. I love you more than you'll ever know."

At Father Sears' prompting, I committed Jeremy into Jesus' eternal care. One day I would be with them both, but for now, Jeremy had to rest in Jesus' arms. And to Jesus I said, "I know Your love for him is so much greater than my own. Lord, I trust You to care for my son."

In the silence that followed the committal service, my

crying continued. They were unbridled tears of joy. Father Sears sat quietly with me until the tears finally stopped. I will be forever grateful for that wonderful committal service he provided for me.

And for little Jeremy.

On my flight back to Portland I was amazed at the exhilaration I felt. Now my child was not an anonymous, dim memory. He had a name and I knew that he was experiencing eternal life with my Lord. I knew this was the final closure of my abortion experience. I had not even been aware that I'd needed it all these years.

The only thing that gave me any pause in returning to my work with my clients was Betty. I knew she was not psychotic and could truly distinguish between the imaginary and the physical world. Could something like this committal service possibly lift the load she seemed to bear?

When Betty arrived for her next appointment, I suggested we try an inner healing journey. I explained the relevant details to her.

She shrugged with the same flatness she always showed. "Okay. I don't think I'll ever forgive myself for killing my baby, but if you think we should try it. . . ."

Guiding her through the memory of her younger days was painful indeed. The specifics of her abortion were sad. Hers had been performed by a rather shady doctor "after hours." She had sneaked in under cover of darkness and left in both physical and emotional pain that was excruciating. First she feared she would die. Then she feared she would *live*.

When we got to the part where Jesus entered the room

with her, my heart was in my throat. Sitting with her eyes closed, she looked like a broken doll, forgotten in a corner. Vulnerable. *O Jesus,* I prayed, *make this real for her. I know You're her last hope.*

She drew a sharp breath. "Oh, Susan—He's here. I was sure He wouldn't come."

"Do you see the baby, Betty?"

Slowly she nodded, a tear trickling down her face. Then, "Oh, my! Wait. I can't believe it. Oh, goodness. . . ."

"Betty," I urged, "what is it? Tell me what you see."

"Susan, I can't believe it!" Her shoulders were shaking with emotion. "Jesus is holding a baby in each arm. There are *two.*"

This was the first time I'd seen Betty express any emotion. Almost in a whisper, I ventured, "Can you tell the sex? Do you have any sense of their names?"

"A boy . . . and a girl. Fraternal twins. Oh, I can't believe it. Somehow I always had the feeling there were two. My little Jonathan—and little Joanie."

For a time I allowed her to bask in the silence with her babies. Then I led her through a committal service like the one Father Sears had done with me. In the name of the Father, and of the Son, and of the Holy Spirit, we committed Jonathan and Joan into Jesus' tender arms for all eternity. What a magnificent surge went through me when I spoke the final words that came to me in prayer: "Betty, you are forgiven—and free. The Lord loves you and your children."

When we finished, the "double-heaviness" that had plagued Betty had lifted. She left that day, a woman at the beginning of a new path—a path of healing, freedom, and new life. There were still many questions to answer as she sorted out her options, but the smile that had replaced the frozen deadness on her face said it all. Now she could begin to believe in herself. Hope had taken the place of hopelessness.

That evening I spent two hours thanking God for the clear direction He had given me, for the hardness of the path on which He had led me—and for the incredible rewards I was seeing in the lives of women like Jacqueline and Betty. No longer would I be timid in dealing with women suffering from the aftereffects of abortion. He had taken the darkest experience of my life and turned it into a means of healing. And for all those women who were open spiritually to be touched by the living God, I knew there was an answer. Jesus was and is the great Healer of all time.

Since those first days of my inner healing work with grieving post-abortion women, I have continued to witness the Lord's mighty healing power touching so many. One of the most dramatic cases I've worked with is that of a woman I'll call Cory. She was referred to me by her physician after she'd complained of severe anxiety attacks, nervousness, and an irregular heartbeat.

Cory's physician expressed to me his belief that her physical problems were a manifestation of psychosomatic illness. "She certainly is showing physical strain and severe anxiety," he said during the referral phone call. "But I feel their cause rests in the psychological area. I would rather not medicate her," he said. "Perhaps you can determine what is really underlying all her stress?"

"I'd be glad to see her," I volunteered, "and I'll keep you apprised of what we find."

Cory presented herself in my office extremely well turned out but obviously highly anxious. As I began my initial intake interview Cory explained why she thought she was suffering so much anxiety. "You see my husband and I are having some struggles regarding parenthood. He is thirty-three and really wants to become a father. He's worried that he'll be too old when the kids are growing up.

"On the other hand I'm only twenty-three and I'm not sure I'm ready to be a mom. It's a lot of responsibility and I don't know if I can handle it." She continually fidgeted with a bracelet she'd taken off her wrist and avoided much eye contact with me.

Then the real impact on her physical condition unfolded. "You see," she continued, "I've already suffered two miscarriages since we've been married and now I'm not sure I want to be a mother at all."

"Tell me more about the situations of your miscarriages, Cory."

"Well, the first one happened two years ago but I was only two months pregnant. I felt a little sad about it, but it was not too bad. About eight months after that, at my husband's insistence, I got pregnant again. I was determined that this time everything would be okay. . . ."

Tears flooded her dark brown eyes as she stared at the now quiet bracelet in her hand. "But I lost her anyway. I went all the way to the end of my fifth month and then one day soon after breakfast I felt the contractions begin. . . ."

Now her tears had evolved to real crying. "I guess I'm just not fit to be a mother," she said as she finished.

It was clear to me that her psychological ambivalence about being a mother was affecting her physical ability to carry her babies. Over the next three months Cory and I developed a trusting therapeutic relationship wherein Cory was able to work through her grief regarding her two lost babies.

During that time I learned that her own faith, while new, was developing as a result of her husband's strong involvement with his church. I suggested we do a committal prayer for each of her miscarried children and explained its relevance and the peace it brings. Now I offer this to all women who've had miscarried, stillborn, or aborted babies and who believe in an afterlife. They reach such peace seeing their babies in the arms of Jesus.

After we had gone through each of the steps that were relevant for Cory, I had a nudging sense that there was still something not yet shared that was blocking a total healing in this case. Our rapport was well enough established now that I gently ventured my observation. The following result could not have been more dramatic. Cory suddenly burst into tears and continued to sob holding her head in her hands. Expressing relief through her tears, she said she realized that she had to confide in someone. Not even her doctors knew. Prior to being married she had gotten pregnant twice and had chosen to have abortions in both cases.

Since her marriage and coming to develop a faith in Jesus she was feeling tremendous guilt at having aborted both babies. I helped her to see how her guilt about her abortions and her anxiety attacks were all intertwined with her two subsequent miscarriages.

We then began to focus our work on Jesus being a loving, forgiving, and healing God. I helped her to grasp the power 'and impact available in understanding the true depth of God's kindness. Once we had explored the fullness of the forgiveness that Jesus offers us, Cory began to realize that she could forgive herself. I conducted two separate inner healing journeys for each of Cory's aborted babies, ending with a committal prayer for each one.

Then at the end of all our work God gave us an incredible example of His love. Cory saw the most beautiful scene in her mind's eye during our prayer journeys. "Susan, it takes my breath away—it's so beautiful. There is so much peace and love there. Jesus is sitting in a field of long grass. And you won't believe this, but there are four little children playing with Him in that field. They are climbing on His back, tumbling over His shoulder, and falling in and out of His lap. There is so much love and laughter present. . . . It's the most beautiful thing I've ever seen. I know that my four children are with Jesus now for all eternity, and I'll get to meet them in heaven."

The peace on her face said it most of all. Gone were the anxious darting eyes, the ever-fidgety fooling with something in her hands. Her whole persona portrayed a new tranquility. Cory's children were at home and she could be at peace. Eleven months after our last session Cory delivered a healthy 9½-pound baby boy!

Yes, Jesus *is* the great Healer of all time.

A FINAL THOUGHT

My journey has brought me to several discoveries that have been key to my own healing. Primarily, I've learned that God loves us unconditionally. He is always waiting patiently for us to turn to Him so He can greet us with His loving, open arms. And He wants to heal us.

Just as Jesus brought the healing love of His Father to so many when He was on this earth, He told his followers to go and do the same: "Believe me when I say that I am in the Father and the Father is in me. . . . I tell you the truth, anyone who has faith in me will do what I have been doing. He will do even greater things than these, because I am going to the Father. And I will do whatever you ask in my name, so that the Son may bring glory to the Father" (John 14:11–13). Jesus does heal today and I believe He wishes to forgive and heal every woman who has had an abortion.

Jesus' healing brings with it an inner peace and happiness that far surpass any human understanding. No money or riches or fame of this world can ever bring the kind of peace and tranquility that a personal relationship with Jesus can bring to our hearts.

With this healing and love comes a directive. We can think of love as one side of a golden coin: What makes it so valuable and powerful is that the other side of the coin is *forgiveness*. We are told to forgive with the measure that we have been forgiven. I believe that love can never reach its full potential if we do not use a great measure of forgiveness in our dealings with others—those we have hurt, and those who have hurt us.

My own healing has been complete because of my understanding of how much God loves me and has forgiven me. In a similar way my healing reached greater fruition as I dealt with the issue of forgiveness between my father and me, as well as between my former husband and myself. In many ways these were the hardest people for me to forgive in my entire life. But the mandate from Jesus is clear. As we are forgiven so we must forgive.

Through obedience to the Lord and fully letting go of old hurts, I've come to know a peace within that far surpasses anything the world can give. It was certainly not by my own doing but purely by the grace of God that I was able to let go completely and forgive. It has put the final cap on my healing.

12
HEALING STEPS FOR POST-ABORTION TRAUMA

1. Awareness of the "Unfinished Business."

The counselor comes to the realization that the pain expressed by the client may actually be related to "unfinished business" or aftermath from the client's abortion experience. This may be reflected by the client's indication that she has repeated annual depressions around the time of her abortion or the potential birth date of her child. Other presenting complaints might reflect generalized depression or unhappiness. Sometimes this might be presented as related to the decision to abort and other times not so. It is impossible to be totally comprehensive regarding all consequent emotions, but any trained counselor or therapist will quickly recognize the common emotions associated with grieving and depression. Sometimes the client will state very simply: "I'm not sure I can ever forgive

161

myself for having had my abortion," and thus the problem is clearly defined.

2. Link to Abortion Identified.

The counselor needs to suggest gently to the client the possibility that the presenting feeling may be due to unfinished business relating to the abortion. The manner in which this is done is crucial. It is important never to "tell" the client that is the problem. Rather, good counseling is best served by the counselor's presenting the idea and asking the client whether that explanation seems to fit. Each client then has an opportunity to respond as to whether her problem may be related to the abortion. I have never seen a woman who was "joyous" about her abortion, even if she does try to rationalize the morality of her decision.

3. General Catharsis of Details.

Once it has been determined that there is some post-abortion aftermath that needs to be dealt with, a detailed enumeration of the facts around the abortion decision should be gathered. There should also be a general catharsis of the feelings involved around the decision. This catharsis will vary in time frame from client to client. The counselor needs to be prepared to spend whatever number of sessions it takes to finish getting a full enumeration of all the relevant facts and emotions relating to the abortion experience. This is important so that when the healing of the memories experience is done, the counselor will have a clear idea of just which emotions are important to focus on during the healing prayer.

4. Spiritual Frame of Reference.

At some point during the gathering of historical data, the counselor needs to ascertain a clear definition of the client's spiritual frame of reference. How does she view God? Does she see God as "somebody with a big flyswatter in the sky"? Or does she believe God is a loving and forgiving Father? In my own counseling practice, about 80 percent of the people coming to me express some degree of belief in God. However, how they view Him is an important element and needs to be enunciated. The counselor can offer to the client the concept that God is a loving Father who wants His children healed. Forgiveness is ours for the asking. Sometimes the client will express some skepticism or disbelief that God could want to heal or forgive what she has found so difficult to forgive in herself. My explanation, then, is that experience is the best teacher and that we need to trust God jointly. Do not judge the client. Simply explain Jesus' desire for her to be forgiven and healed, and then accept her where she is at the present time. Sometimes it takes a while for her to change her focus of God from an authoritative figure to a loving Friend.

5. The Blending of Psychology with Christianity.

The counselor needs to spend some time educating the client to the interweaving of psychology and the tenets of Christian healing. In my work I explain to my clients that the science of psychology is aimed at helping individuals learn to overcome and deal with difficult events in their lives, but I do not believe that psychology alone is the answer. For those clients of mine who express a belief in Christ, I spend some time explaining to them how Jesus wishes for us to be healed today. I believe Jesus commands that His followers go out and heal as He did, using His name and the power that comes from Him. (See John 14:12.) It is important to spend sufficient time at this stage helping the client understand that Jesus heals just as powerfully today as when He walked this earth 2,000 years ago. Psychology offers only adjustment and "working through" traumatic events. Jesus, however, can provide us with total healing. In the healing of the memories exercise we use the trusted psychological tool of guided imagery and interweave it with the presence of our almighty Lord.

6. Client Chooses Yes or No.

At this stage the counselor explains the concept of the healing of the memories exercise to the client and how the procedure unfolds. The role Jesus plays in touching and healing the memory of her painful abortion is delineated. I indicate that tears may come more often than not, but that it is helpful to let them flow, as they are often an important element of the healing experience. I then offer the client an opportunity to have any questions answered she may have. From there the client can choose whether or not she is ready to proceed. If the experience has been presented in a timely fashion, the client is usually ready to go ahead. An important aspect in timing is whether the client has someone she has not yet been able to forgive related to her abortion. Lack of forgiveness is one of the few issues I've seen get in the way of a successful healing of the memories experience.

7. Beginning with Prayer to Jesus as Healer.

The healing of the memories experience should always be started with a prayer giving all the glory to God. Something like the following is appropriate: "Heavenly Father, we thank You for Your promise that when two or more are gathered in Your name, You are in our midst. We thank You for Your presence here with us, and we ask You to be the head of our ship as we journey toward healing for this client. In the name of Jesus, I bind any spirits of darkness that would try to distract or take us off course from the healing we are seeking. Jesus, I know You to be the one true Healer from whom all total healing comes, whether through medicine, psychology, or divine healing. We thank You for the healing You are already doing, and that which You will continue to do with this client. Guide us now, Holy Spirit, so that this client will receive total forgiveness and healing from her abortion. May all the glory be Yours. Amen."

8. Healing of the Abortion Memory.

After the beginning prayer is finished, I use the psychological concept of a guided imagery to lead the client back to the painful memory. I ask her to choose a comfortable posture, close her eyes, bow her head, and relax so that the details in her memory can unfold. "I would like you now, 'Jane,' to let yourself journey back in your memory to that time around your abortion experience. Allow the Holy Spirit to run the projector of your memory. Perhaps some particular part of the event will stand out to you, like the abortion clinic, or where you were when you made the decision to have the abortion, or perhaps your feelings after you had the abortion. It is different for each individual. Just allow your mind to open up and visualize your memories." After a few moments' pause I then ask: "Can you tell me what has come to your mind at this point?"

Usually the client then explains where she sees herself in her memory and who else might be present. She continues to do this with her eyes closed, focusing mostly on the memory, but sharing her surroundings with me.

"Fine, Jane, that's very good. Now, I would like you to allow yourself not only to get in touch with the facts and the circumstances around your decision, but more importantly, to start to sense the breadth of feelings that were present at that time. Spend a few moments now concentrating on your emotions. If you want to cry, let the tears flow."

Once again, I allow the client to have some moments of silence to focus in on her feelings. Frequently the client may begin to cry as she gets in touch with the sadness around her abortion. Initially it is soft crying, but it is an important part of the grieving and healing process. Not all clients cry, however, and this should not be seen as a prerequisite in order for healing to take place.

"Now, Jane, in your memory I'd like you to look up from wherever you are sitting or lying and look over to the nearest doorway. I'd like you to see, standing at that door, what you would imagine a loving, forgiving, and healing Jesus to look like. He may be tall or short, He may or may not have a beard, but I want you to imagine Him as you think Jesus would look. He is probably wearing a long white robe and you notice that He has a very loving smile on His face. He seems to be radiating a deep warmth and love and there appears to be no judgment or scorn anywhere on His face.

"Then you also notice as you see Him standing there that He is holding something in His arms. It is something wrapped in a blanket, and after a moment or two you realize that He is holding a little baby. He is holding your baby, Jane, and He loves it just as much as you would if that baby were right here on earth with you. Now I want you to get up and go across the room in your memory and face Jesus where He is standing. You look straight at Him, and He holds your gaze with His forgiving eyes. You realize that Jesus is not condemning you. He is only loving you. His death on the Cross was to atone for all of our sins, so He stands there offering you forgiveness and love. The gentle smile on His face never leaves, and you begin to feel His permeating love flowing deep into your heart and mind. I want you now just to drink in His love and allow it to come inside your whole being.

"I am going to be quiet for a few minutes, and I want you to dialogue with Jesus in silence. Give Him all of your pain. Tell Him about all the feelings and emotions that you have—every single one of them. Lay all of your hurt and sadness at His feet; give Him every feeling that is present for you. Then, when you are finished telling Him about all of your feelings, I want you to be quiet. Jesus has some things He wants to say to you and I want you to listen to Him. He may say just a word or two, or He may give you several sentences. You will come to realize His words are full of healing power. They are His healing touch to you. Each message He gives is individual to each person. As you are journeying in your dialogue with Jesus, I will be in silent prayer holding you up to our loving Father."

Again, leave the client alone with the Lord for five or ten minutes to dialogue with Jesus. The majority of the time the client will cry. I have seen some women break down and sob. I do not stop this, for I know it is part of the healing process. I continue to pray in silence to our almighty Lord. Often I will ask the Holy Spirit to guide my prayers, trusting that He can express best my prayer of petition for healing for my client. It's important to note that all of this should be done in silence, so as not to distract the client in her own journey and healing experience with Jesus.

9. Committal Service of the Baby.

After I have left the client alone with the Lord for five to ten minutes (this may vary depending on the client), I ask if she is ready to share with me what has transpired during her dialogue with Jesus. She remains seated in a contemplative posture while she describes what has happened. I write down verbatim what she tells me. The reason for this is that I ask her to reread this page daily for the following one or two weeks. It is my experience that she receives additional healing as she goes back over the words Jesus says to her. These words are, in and of themselves, part of His continuing healing touch on this memory.

After I have written down what transpired, I go back and lead the client in the final part of her healing:

"Lord Jesus, we know that Jane's baby is with You now in heaven. Jane can see her baby being held in Your arms. Lord, we thank You for the love You have for this child and for how You love each one of us individually on this earth. Thank You also, Lord, for all those children who never make it to this earth, either through miscarriage or abortion. We know, Lord, that You love every soul that is created. We want now, Lord, to commit this baby of Jane's to You forever."

At this point I will stop my prayer and ask Jane if she has any sense of what the sex of her child might be.

It's absolutely phenomenal how many of my clients do have some inner sense of whether they were going to have a boy or a girl. It does not happen with everyone but certainly with a strong majority of women with whom I've done this healing work.

I then ask if she has any hint of a name the baby might have been called. The client will often blurt out the name of the child "almost from nowhere." Often days or weeks later she will tell me she was so surprised to hear herself say that name because it was not a name that she would have "chosen" for her child. I do not pretend to explain this phenomenon; I simply report that it happens. It appears as if it was the child's name for eternity! After we have gleaned these two pieces of information I continue my prayer:

"Heavenly Father, Lord Jesus, and Holy Spirit, we come to You at this point in our journey and we wish to dedicate this child to You for all eternity. We know, Lord, that You love this child more than any earthly parent can comprehend. But Jane, as the earthly parent of this child, wishes now to commit her daughter to You forever. In the name of the Father, and of the Son, and of the Holy Spirit, we commit little 'Janie' to You, heavenly Father, to be with You in heaven, to be loved by You, and to be with Your host of angels for all time. Thank You, Father, for the love that You have for this child. We ask you to keep her safe from any darkness or evil and to keep her fully in the presence of Your light in heaven. We are confident, Lord, that one day the souls of Jane and her daughter will be joined together in heaven and we look forward to that day. We praise You, Father, and we thank You for all the healing that you are doing at this very moment."

I then conclude by asking Jane if she has anything she would like to add to the prayer and committal service of her daughter, and that she may choose to do that either out loud, or silently if she's more comfortable that way. I also ask her to listen silently for a few moments to any final words that she may sense from her Lord or from the soul of her baby. This is also a very powerful healing moment. It usually is one in which an indescribable love is exchanged between both mother and child. Sometimes words of forgiveness are also exchanged. At the appropriate time, I close this final part of the service with a prayer:

"Lord Jesus, we praise You and we thank You for all that You have just done to heal Jane of her abortion. We thank You for little Janie, and for Your taking care of her for eternity. We thank You also, Lord, for how Your death and resurrection have set us free from all our sins. We thank You for the new freedom Jane feels. Father, I ask You to carry Jane in the palm of Your hand for this week until we meet again. Continue her healing. Help her to continue to see the power of Your love and Your healing forgiveness. We praise You, in Jesus' name. Amen."

Resource List
for Further Reference

Gardner, R. F. R., M.D. *Abortion: The Personal Dilemma.* Old Tappan, N.J.: Spire Books, 1972.

Hilgers, Thomas; Horan, Dennis; and Mall, David, eds. *New Perspectives on Human Abortion.* Washington, D.C.: University Publications of America, 1981.

Lake, Frank. *Tight Corners in Pastoral Counseling.* London: Darton, Longman & Todd, 1981.

Mall, David and Watts, Walter, eds. *The Psychological Aspects of Abortion.* Washington, D.C.: University Publications of America, 1979.

McAll, Kenneth, M.D. *Healing the Family Tree.* London: Sheldon Publishing, 1982.

Montagu, Ashley. *Life Before Birth.* New York: Signet Publications, 1965.

Nathanson, Bernard, M.D. and Ostling, Richard. *Aborting America.* New York: Doubleday, 1979.

Powell, John, S. J. *Abortion: The Silent Holocaust.* Texas: Argus Communications, 1981.

Rosen, Harold, ed. *Abortion in America.* Boston: Beacon Press, 1967.

Verny, Thomas, M.D. *The Secret Life of the Unborn Child.* New York: Dell Publishing, 1981.

Willke, Dr. & Mrs. John. *Handbook on Abortion,* revised edition. Cincinnati: Hayes Publishing, 1975.

Woody, Jeanine. *Abortion?* Texas: Hunter Ministries Publishing, 1977.

A. A. PREGNANCY HELP CENTER
1309 SOUTH LIMESTONE
LEXINGTON, KENTUCKY
278-8469   40503